Also by JAMES L. W. WEST III

AMERICAN AUTHORS AND
THE LITERARY MARKETPLACE

WILLIAM STYRON, A LIFE

THE PERFECT HOUR

Hq. Co. 45th Inf.
Camp Sheridan Ala
July 21st, 1'1

you
Mitchell
heard
be one
        Doe
igh w
ettled
the m
marryi

Scott

The

PERFECT HOUR

THE ROMANCE OF

F. SCOTT FITZGERALD

and GINEVRA KING,

HIS FIRST LOVE

. . .

JAMES L. W. WEST III

RANDOM HOUSE | NEW YORK

Copyright © 2005 by James L. W. West III

Published in the United States by Random House,
an imprint of The Random House Publishing Group,
a division of Random House, Inc., New York.

RANDOM HOUSE and colophon are registered
trademarks of Random House, Inc.

Library of Congress Cataloging-in-Publication Data

West III, James L. W.
The perfect hour: the romance of F. Scott Fitzgerald and
Ginevra King / by James L. W. West III.—1st ed.
p. cm.
Includes bibliographical references and index.
ISBN 1-4000-6308-6 (alk. paper)
1. Fitzgerald, F. Scott (Francis Scott), 1896–1940—Relations
with women.   2. Authors, American—20th century—
Biography.   3. King, Ginevra, 1898–1980.   I. Title.
PS3511.I9Z918 2005
813'.52—dc22
[B]   2004051088

Random House website address: www.atrandom.com

Printed in the United States of America on acid-free paper

246897531

FIRST EDITION

Book design by Barbara M. Bachman

*Frontispiece: Photo of F. Scott Fitzgerald and facsimile of his last letter to Ginevra King,
Princeton University Libraries. Photo of Ginevra King, courtesy of Ginevra M. Hunter.*

For my mother,

KATE B. WEST

A C K N O W L E D G M E N T S

I am grateful to Ginevra Hunter, Ginevra Chandler, and Cynthia Hunter for sharing their memories of Ginevra King with me. Ginevra Hunter has kindly granted permission to quote from her mother's letters and diary.

My thanks to Don Skemer, Curator of Manuscripts at Princeton University Library, for bringing Ginevra's letters and diary to my attention, and to AnnaLee Pauls, Margaret Sherry Rich, Charles Greene, and Ben Primer in the Department of Rare Books and Special Collections at Princeton for assistance with facsimiles and permissions.

My article-length account of the romance between Scott and Ginevra appeared in the Fall 2003 issue of the *Princeton University Library Chronicle;* I thank that journal and its editor, Gretchen Oberfranc, for permission to reprint portions of the article here, and for other assistance. Rosemary Switzer and Tad Bennicoff at the Seeley G. Mudd Manuscript Library, Princeton University, located and copied surviving photos of *The Evil Eye*. Thomas P. Roche, Jr., Emeritus Professor of English at Princeton, was most hospitable to me during my visits to the university.

For information about Lake Forest and photographs of the King and Mitchell residences there, I thank Elizabeth Hedsund of the

Lake Forest/Lake Bluff Historical Society and Arthur H. Miller of Lake Forest College.

Piriya Metcalfe of the Chicago Historical Society helped with images and permissions from the *Tribune* records. Harry Maurer at The Free Library of Philadelphia and Nancy Down at the Browne Popular Culture Library, Bowling Green State University, collaborated in supplying the *Metropolitan* text of "Winter Dreams."

Eleanor Lanahan, Fitzgerald's granddaughter, kindly provided a photograph of his Triangle Club watch charm. The following people at Westover School were most helpful: Richard J. Beebe, the Director of Publications; Maria Randall Allen, the school archivist; and Laurie Lisle, who is writing a history of Westover.

George Bornstein, Chris Clausen, Beth Luey, Scott Donaldson, Mary Lee Carns, and Ruth Prigozy read the manuscript of this book and offered useful suggestions. Thanks to Robert Caserio, my department head at Penn State, and to Susan Welch, my dean, for their continuing support.

I am grateful to my research assistants, Jeanne Alexander and Rob Bleil, for extended labors in the library and on the Internet, and to Jeanne for a careful reading of the manuscript.

J. L.W. W. III

CONTENTS

"Honestly and truly, it would be wonderful
to have that perfect hour, sometime,
someday and somewhere."
— GINEVRA TO SCOTT,
January 31, 1916

. . .

Ginevra King was F. Scott Fitzgerald's first great love. She was a petite, beautiful, socially poised teenager from Lake Forest, Illinois, a community of gracefully curving streets, wide lawns, large houses, and carefully cultivated gardens located along the shores of Lake Michigan about thirty miles north of Chicago. Scott met Ginevra on January 4, 1915, at a party in his hometown of St. Paul, Minnesota. On that evening they began an intense romance, largely epistolary, that flourished for six months and lasted for two years. Scott never forgot the experience: Ginevra became the model for many of his fictional heroines—characters who helped to define the behavior and attitudes of young American women during the 1920s and early 1930s. A short list of these characters includes Isabelle Borgé and Rosalind Connage in *This Side of Paradise* (1920), Kismine Washington in "The Diamond as Big as the Ritz" (1922), Judy Jones in

"Winter Dreams" (1922), Minnie Bibble in the Basil Duke Lee stories (1928–29), Josephine Perry in the Josephine stories (1930–31), and, most important, Daisy Buchanan in *The Great Gatsby* (1925).

Arthur Mizener and Andrew Turnbull, Fitzgerald's first two biographers, were aware of Ginevra's importance. They approached her for the story of her romance with Scott, but she was reticent and evasive. Scott Fitzgerald had been only one of many boys who had pursued her, she said. Theirs had been a youthful infatuation; she had destroyed his letters, at his request, when the romance ended. Ginevra corresponded with Mizener, whose life of Fitzgerald, *The Far Side of Paradise,* was published in 1951. She also gave some information to Turnbull for *Scott Fitzgerald,* a book that appeared in 1962, but she spoke to none of the other Fitzgerald biographers, despite the fact that she lived until 1980, well into the revival of interest in his life and career. Perhaps as a result she remains a flat figure in the writings about him, a rich girl he pursued and lost before he fell in love with Zelda Sayre, the talented and unconventional woman he married.

Most of Fitzgerald's biographers, early and late, have based their remarks about Ginevra on passages from his fictional portraits of her. Literary biographers often adopt this strategy, but it can be risky. The characters Fitzgerald modeled on Ginevra are beautiful and alluring, but they can also be vain, headstrong, and manipulative. They are capable of romantic attachments and even of love, but they retain an unapologetic self-interest and a cool indifference to the hurt they cause in others. These women are realists, just as most of the male leads in Fitzgerald's writings are romantics. The "Ginevra" characters will risk social reputation for an emotional interlude, but they know the importance of status and wealth, and they understand how social codes operate. In the end they always retreat to the safety of money and high social position. The men who have loved them feel exploited, as if they have been used in romantic dalliances and then discarded.

Isabelle, Rosalind, Kismine, Judy, Minnie, Josephine, Daisy, and the others are immensely effective in Fitzgerald's fiction; they help him set forth some of his greatest themes and most penetrating insights. But are they accurate portraits of Ginevra King? It's a commonplace that authors often begin with real-life models, then transform them into characters who bear only distant resemblances to the originals. What was Ginevra really like? And what exactly happened during her romance with Scott Fitzgerald?

Until now we have had little to go on. For Zelda Sayre, the most important woman in Fitzgerald's life, we have had an abundance of material: her letters, manuscripts, and published writings; her paintings and other artwork; records of her medical treatment; testimony from her family and friends. No such body of information has existed for Ginevra King. In April 2003, however, one of Ginevra's granddaughters, Ginevra King Chandler, came upon full transcriptions of her grandmother's letters to Scott in a box of family papers. In the same box, Giny Chandler found the original of Scott's last letter to her grandmother and the private diary that her grandmother had kept during the romance.

Giny had first seen these items as a teenager. She had found them on a back shelf in one of her grandmother's closets—the one in which the evening dresses were kept, for Ginevra King Pirie (as she was then known) always dressed for dinner. Giny asked her grandmother if she might read the diary and letters. No indeed, she was told—those were private. The items were replaced on the closet shelf and stayed there until Ginevra Pirie died in 1980. They were then given to Giny, who put them away, still without reading them.

Giny had almost forgotten them; then they surfaced in a move. Together with her mother and sister, Giny decided in August 2003 to
donate the letters and diary to the Department of Rare Books and
Special Collections at Princeton University Library. They are kept
there now with Fitzgerald's own extensive literary papers, and they
are the basis for this book.*

Ginevra King's letters and diary tell us a great deal about her. She
emerges much more fully and favorably than before: we can now understand her attraction to Scott and his to her, and we can follow the
progress of their romance and learn why it ended as it did. The romance, we now know, was much more than a shallow flirtation.
Ginevra was entirely taken by Scott and he by her. She was drawn to
him by his intelligence and charm, and she admired his talent with
words. He was different from the other young men who pursued her;
she was flattered by his attention and beguiled by his letters.

The relationship was strong and intense on both sides, especially
in its first six months. Ginevra wrote to Scott as frequently as he did
to her, and her letters reveal much about her personality. She was
more complex and likeable than the characters Fitzgerald later based
on her. She was perceptive about him: she knew that he was idealizing her and urged him in her letters not to do so, but of course he
did. Ginevra was pleased by Scott's attention, but she was put off by
his attempts to analyze her personality and by his persistent jealousy. These two factors, more than any others, caused their romance to end.

After it was over Ginevra had to grow up quickly, as did many
members of her generation. The United States entered World War I

---

* For a news story about the donation, see Dinitia Smith, "Love Notes Drenched
in Moonlight," *New York Times*, September 8, 2003, Arts Section, B1ff.

in the spring of 1917; Ginevra married during the war, at nineteen years of age, and by the spring of 1920 was a young mother. She never forgot Scott Fitzgerald, though, and she probably understood him better than he thought she did.

GINEVRA'S LETTERS to Scott are typed transcriptions of the originals, made on his order. When and why he had these transcripts made is not known. The original letters do not survive; it's likely that they were discarded after the transcripts had been typed. In a letter dated July 7, 1917, Ginevra asked Scott to destroy her letters: probably he did so—but only after they had been copied. Thus he would have fulfilled her request without losing the substance of the letters. Having the letters transcribed might also have objectified them, making it easier for him to think of them as documents—as raw material for fiction. He did the same with the diaries that Zelda had kept as a teenager. He had those diaries typed up in 1920, thinking at first to have them published under her name. When that project did not materialize, he used the transcripts to capture Zelda's personality in some of his short stories. He also borrowed passages from them for his 1922 novel, *The Beautiful and Damned*.

Fitzgerald placed the transcripts of Ginevra's letters, which run to 227 double-spaced pages, in a black loose-leaf ring binder. The first page reads "Strictly Private and Personal Letters: Property of F. Scott Fitzgerald (Not Manuscript)." The words "Property of F. Scott Fitzgerald" suggest that, in his mind at least, he had taken possession of the letters. The parenthetical words "Not Manuscript" make it clear, however, that he did not write the letters and did not want them mistakenly published as his own work—by a literary executor, perhaps. Fitzgerald kept the bound transcripts with him

STRICTLY PRIVATE AND PERSONAL LETTERS

Property of

F. SCOTT FITZGERALD

(Not manuscript)

Initial page of the letter transcripts.

throughout his working life and, as we shall see, drew on them for plots and ideas. When he died in December 1940 they were among his literary papers, most of which were donated to Princeton by his daughter, Scottie, early in 1951. She had withheld the transcripts of the letters, however, and in December 1950 had returned them to Ginevra King Pirie, whom she knew through her mother-in-law, Eleanor Lanahan. That is how the transcripts came to be in Ginevra's closet.

The diary, which never left Ginevra's hands, has a different history. It appears to have been given to her as a Christmas gift in 1911, when she was thirteen years old. No numerals for years are printed on its pages—only "January 1," "January 2," and so on. Thus the diary could be used in any year; the diarist had simply to write the year on the page each time an entry was made. Ginevra made only a scattering of entries in 1912 and 1913 and did not begin to keep the diary with any regularity until the fall of 1914. In January 1915, just after she had met Scott, she began to write in it faithfully every night. Not surprisingly, these were the months in which her romance with him was at its most intense.

Ginevra's handwriting in the diary is revealing. On a given page one often finds specimens of her script from more than one year. A handwritten entry from 1913 or 1914, for example, might not fill a page, so she will use the remaining space a year or two later. The handwriting changes—from girlish, rounded letters in the earlier entries to a distinctively feminine hand by 1915. One can see that Ginevra is growing older and maturing simply by looking at the pages of her diary.

To write a complete narrative of this romance one would need Scott's letters to Ginevra. They no longer survive, alas, but a great deal can be learned from what remains—from Ginevra's letters and diary and from other evidence. In this book I will attempt to reconstruct the story of the romance between these two young people. It was an experience that changed them both and supplied Fitzgerald with material that he would write about for his entire literary career.

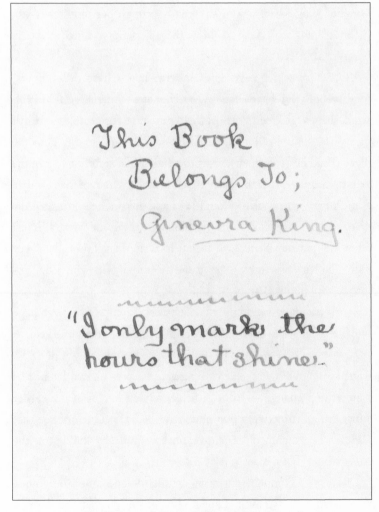

The first page of Ginevra's diary. The quoted words
are often found on sundials.

THE PERFECT HOUR

CHAPTER ONE

Ginevra and Scott

꧁✼꧂

G inevra King was the eldest of the three daughters of Charles Garfield King, a wealthy Chicago stockbroker, and Ginevra Fuller King, his wife. There was money on both sides of the family, earned by Ginevra's grandfathers, both of whom were self-made men. Her paternal grandfather, Charles Bohan King, had come to Chicago from upstate New York in 1863. At first he worked as a wholesale grocer, then as a jobber in hats, caps, and furs. He eventually moved into banking and prospered, retiring in 1885 as president of the Commercial Safe Deposit Co. He was a Republican and a Presbyterian; he sent his older son, Rockwell King, to Harvard and his younger son (Ginevra's father) to Yale.

Ginevra's maternal grandfather, William Alden Fuller, was a native of Massachusetts. He began his working life in 1852 as a station agent for the Worcester & Nashua Railroad; in 1854 he came to Chicago and entered the lumber trade as a bookkeeper. Twelve years later, with backing from Potter Palmer, the dry goods magnate, he struck out as a dealer in building materials. He formed the corporation of Palmer, Fuller & Co.; the business was a success, and he became wealthy during the commercial boom that followed the Civil War. He belonged to the Episcopal Church and the Union League. Ginevra, as a teenager, knew him as a widower who lived in a large house at 2913 Michigan Avenue.

Ginevra's mother and father had married in January 1898, four years after he had taken his degree at Yale. When he wed Ginevra Fuller, Charles King was still a mortgage banker at Shanklin &

Ginevra's father,
Charles Garfield King,
in polo gear.

King, a business backed by his father's money, but in 1900, when Ginevra turned two, he began working on the side as a stockbroker. In 1906 he became a full-time broker, organizing the firm of King,

Farnum & Co., of which he was senior member. The brokerage prospered, operating from seats on both the Chicago and the New York exchanges. He and his wife and children were still living with her father in the house on Michigan Avenue when Ginevra met

Ginevra's home in Lake Forest, called "Kingdom Come Farm."

Scott, but Charles King had already acquired a large summer residence (which he called "Kingdom Come Farm") in Lake Forest, and he was building an elegant four-story mansion in the city at the corner of Astor and Burton.

Charles King and his wife belonged to Onwentsia, an exclusive country club in Lake Forest, where he played golf and polo. He built his own string of polo ponies, which he stabled on his Lake Forest property, and he played for the club in competitions against other teams during the 1890s and early 1900s. The Kings socialized with the other prominent families in Chicago—the Swifts, Armours,

Cudahys, Palmers, McCormicks, and Chatfield-Taylors. The children of these families went to schools and churches together and played with one another in Lake Forest during the summers. Their parents sent them to fashionable New England prep schools; the sons usually stayed in the East to attend Harvard or Yale. This was a tightly knit community: its members were held together by money, property, shared values, and high social status.

The Chicago of the early twentieth century, their Chicago, had been defined by three important events in the last third of the nineteenth century: the Great Chicago Fire of 1871, the Haymarket

The King house on Astor Street in Chicago.

Square Bombing of 1886, and the World's Columbian Exposition of 1893. The fire had destroyed the old city, a prosperous but poorly laid-out center of railroading, meatpacking, and shipping, and had given Chicago's entrepreneurs an opportunity to erect a modern metropolis, with a transportation loop and with some of the world's first skyscrapers. The Haymarket Square Bombing and the riots that followed had set unions and laborers against capitalists in bitter conflicts that lasted well into the twentieth century. Most of the workers were immigrants (many were Irish), and virtually all of them belonged to the Catholic Church, which was thought to have fomented much of the labor agitation. The Columbian Exposition with its famous "White City"—a collection of fanciful, alabaster-colored buildings covering forty-four square acres—was an announcement to the world that Chicago had arrived. The exposition featured an Electricity Building, a Ferris wheel, a reproduction of one of Columbus's ships, a prototype of the movie projector, and a sixty-foot cannon that could fire a shell over sixteen miles. More than twenty-seven million people came to Chicago to visit this exposition; most of them went away convinced that the city was a wonderful example of American hustle, ambition, and commercial power. This was the city in which Ginevra King's family, and other families of the Chicago haute bourgeoisie, were prospering.

GINEVRA WAS THE third woman in her family to bear that given name.* Like her mother and grandmother, she was named for

---

* Ginevra's maternal grandmother was Ginevra Fuller (d. 1888); her mother was Ginevra Fuller King (d. 1964). Ginevra Mitchell Hunter (b. 1926) is her daughter; the elder of Ginevra Hunter's two daughters is Ginevra King Chandler (b. 1954).

Ginevra de Benci, the pensive young Florentine noblewoman of Leonardo da Vinci's famous portrait, painted in 1474 and familiar to nineteenth-century art students and connoisseurs from etchings and oil reproductions.

Ginevra King had a clear sense of her family's wealth and position and, from an early age, a highly developed understanding of how social status worked. During the summer of 1914, in an act of arrogance that could probably only be managed by a group of pretty fifteen-year-old girls, Ginevra and three of her friends had declared themselves to be the "Big Four"—the four most attractive and socially desirable young women in Chicago. They had not consulted anyone about this; they had simply anointed themselves. The other three girls were Edith Cummings, Courtney Letts, and Margaret ("Peg") Carry. The girls had four identical pinky rings made of rose gold; engraved inside each ring, in script letters, was "*The Big Four 1914.*" (Ginevra's ring can be seen on her right hand, next to a signet ring, in the frontispiece of this book.) The girls went to dances and house parties together, and they were seen as a foursome on the golf links and tennis courts at Onwentsia. If other girls were jealous, Ginevra and her three friends did not care. The Big Four was complete; it would admit no further members.

Ginevra herself was lovely. She was small, about five feet four inches in height, with refined features and a good profile. She had a slim figure, pretty legs and ankles, and small, graceful hands. Her hair was dark and curly; her eyes, deep brown in color, were lively and sparkling. Ginevra's voice was her most unusual attribute— low and expressive, with a slight roughness of texture. She liked to sing and laugh: if something truly amused her she would produce a snort. She loved parties, adored dancing, and was adept in social situations, relying on her looks and instincts to see her through.

Ginevra's diary reveals other things about her. She was intensely competitive and did not like to lose at anything—golf, tennis, or even basketball (for which she was undersized). She loved athletics and was a good enough golfer to hold her own against Edith Cum-

Entry hall for the house on Astor Street.

mings, who later won two national titles in the sport. Ginevra was reasonably diligent about her schoolwork but wasn't terribly interested in it. She preferred athletics and parties, and she liked to sit up late talking with her friends. She was direct in speech and self-

Ginevra's Big Four ring, lying on a page of her diary.
(The ring is worn today by her granddaughter, Cynthia Hunter.)

confident in behavior; there was little that was studied or calculated about what she did or said. She was not especially interested in discussing the shortcomings of others and was not much inclined toward introspection or self-analysis.

When Scott Fitzgerald met her, Ginevra was halfway through her sophomore year at Westover School in Middlebury, Connecticut. Westover, a country boarding school, was a relatively new institution. It had been founded in 1910 by Miss Mary Robbins Hillard and her associate Miss Theodate Pope. Miss Hillard had taught from 1885 to 1891 at Miss Porter's School in Farmington, Connecticut (where Miss Pope had been her student), and had been principal of St. Margaret's in Waterbury for the eighteen years following.

Westover was a small, exclusive finishing school: about 150 girls were enrolled, and their training was focused on languages, literature, history, art, and music. Occasionally Miss Hillard would read

Portrait of Ginevra King, June 1915.

aloud from the newspaper to the girls at assembly, but otherwise the outside world did not intrude. Only five or six of the forty or so graduates each year went on to college. Most of the girls were destined to be the wives of wealthy men; they would find fulfillment in social activities, in child-rearing, and, if they wished to, in helping the needy. This was a point much stressed at Westover; the girls were given a strong sense of social responsibility and American-style noblesse oblige.

Accommodations at Westover were relatively spartan; the emphasis was on character-building. The girls were required to take daily exercise, either in sports or in "jogging," a rapid trotting that was encouraged in the afternoons. Westover had no religious affiliation; most of the students belonged to Protestant denominations and attended churches in Middlebury. Much energy went into singing, plays, picnics, and single-sex dances, which were called "Germans" and were held each Saturday night. Girls attended these dances as couples; crushes between younger and older girls were common.

The dormitory rooms were large and commodious. Maids (all from Trinidad and the Virgin Islands) looked after the laundry and housekeeping chores. Girls often spent the night with one another and stayed awake after lights-out to gossip and talk. Uniforms were required: a khaki skirt with a black patent-leather belt and a white blouse during the day; a white dress with black silk stockings and low-heeled shoes in the evenings. For sports the girls wore black alpaca bloomers, thick black stockings, and Peter Pan blouses. On the coldest days, corduroy deerstalker hats were issued, with flaps to keep one's ears warm. As for cosmetics, only a little face powder was permitted—no lip rouge.

Ginevra did not much like Westover. She was not truly unhappy there, but the close supervision of her academic performance and her behavior seems to have rankled her. She had no special aspirations to excel in her classes; she studied with fair diligence and maintained a B average, but much of the assigned work bored her. The fun outside classes at Westover was not really to her taste. She would have preferred more opportunities to see other teenagers and to go into New York City for plays and amusements. Ginevra had a disobedient streak: she had managed to get herself crosswise with Miss Hillard, who criticized her behavior and summoned her to the office from time to time for lectures on deportment. It's likely that Ginevra, who was as strong-willed as Miss Hillard, rather enjoyed testing the school rules and getting under the skin of its headmistress. Perhaps she told these things to Scott Fitzgerald on the night she met him.

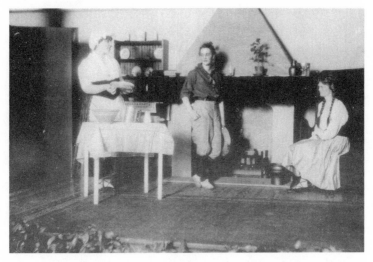

Ginevra, dressed as a boy, performing in a school play at Westover.

F. SCOTT FITZGERALD was the only son of Edward Fitzgerald, a marginally successful wholesale grocery salesman in St. Paul, and Mollie McQuillan Fitzgerald, his wife. There was money in Scott's family, but only on his mother's side and only in the previous generation. Mollie's father, Philip F. McQuillan, had immigrated to America in 1843, at the age of nine, from County Fermanagh in Ireland. He and his parents had settled in Galena, Illinois. His success story resembles the "up-by-the-bootstraps" stories of Ginevra's grandfathers. At the age of twenty-three, Philip moved to St. Paul and took a position as a bookkeeper with Beaupre & Temple, a wholesale grocery house. In 1858 he ventured out on his own in the same business and prospered in the years following the Civil War. Philip McQuillan merged his firm with that of his former employer in 1875 to form McQuillan, Beaupre & Co. Philip was an energetic man with considerable business acumen. He became a respected citizen of St. Paul (a member of the "lace-curtain" Irish, not the "pig-in-the-parlor" Irish) and a generous benefactor of the local Catholic church.

Philip, however, contracted Bright's disease in his late thirties and died in 1878 at the age of forty-four. He left an estate of more than $266,000—a substantial amount at the time. It was enough to support his widow, Louisa McQuillan, for the rest of her life and to keep their children in relative comfort, even as adults. The money, however, did not beget more money as it had in Ginevra's family. The five surviving McQuillan children seemed content to live on the proceeds of their father's estate.

Mollie, the eldest daughter, married Edward Fitzgerald in 1890. Edward was a small, dapper man who had moved to St. Paul in the mid-1870s from Rockville, Maryland. He too was a Catholic, though not a devout one. He was descended from Maryland ancestors who had settled in the colony sometime during the seventeenth century. Edward was a "well-bred" man with excellent Southern manners, but he was short on ambition and business savvy.

Certainly there were opportunities in St. Paul for him to be successful. The city, situated at the navigational head of the Mississippi River, was a prosperous center of commerce, manufacturing, banking, railroading, and insurance. As the state capital, St. Paul boasted handsome government buildings and large hotels, impressive museums and restaurants and theaters. The chief drawback to life there was the frigid winter weather, though St. Paul residents made the most of it, building ice palaces and organizing winter carnivals to break up the monotony of the long cold season.

In the early 1890s, shortly after marrying Mollie McQuillan, Edward Fitzgerald organized the American Rattan & Willow Works, which manufactured wicker furniture. This business (ill-suited, one would think, to the Minnesota climate) failed in 1898. Edward moved with his family to Buffalo, New York, where he took a job as a salesman for Procter & Gamble. He was transferred by the company to Syracuse in 1900, then back to Buffalo in 1903; but in 1908, at the age of fifty-five, he was cut loose permanently and had to return to St. Paul. There he earned a small livelihood as a wholesale grocery salesman, working from a desk in his brother-in-law's real estate firm, making a little money on his own but relying for support primarily on his wife's family. As a boy Scott often heard his mother say, "If it weren't for your Grandfather McQuillan, where would we be now?"

Mollie McQuillan Fitzgerald was a mildly eccentric woman who doted on her son. Her first two children, both daughters, had died in infancy, shortly before Scott's birth in 1896, and she had focused much attention on him when he was young. He had been named Francis Scott Key Fitzgerald after the author of "The Star-Spangled Banner," who was a distant relative on his father's side. Scott was a beautiful boy, with blond hair and arrestingly bright blue-green eyes. He excelled in school plays and at local dramatics, and he showed some literary ability in his early teens, but he was a mediocre athlete and a thoroughly indifferent student.

As Mollie McQuillan's son, Scott was made welcome in the homes of St. Paul's better families. His father's marginal financial status, however, made his social position uncertain. Most of his

Scott and his father, Edward Fitzgerald.

friends lived in large houses on or near Summit Avenue, the show-place residential street; his own parents, by contrast, lived always in rented dwellings—respectable lodgings but not nearly so impressive as the houses of the St. Paul elite. In January 1915, when he met Ginevra, he and his parents were living at 593 Summit Avenue, a rented unit in a large block of brownstones. Social rankings were fluid and relaxed; for the most part St. Paul was still a second-generation city. Scott probably did not need to worry overmuch about his family's social status, but he did so all the same, and tried to compensate by emphasizing his looks and charm.

When Scott met Ginevra, his family lived at 593 Summit Avenue,
a unit in this block of brownstones.

Scott's poor academic performance caused him to be packed off, at fourteen, to the Newman School, a new and not especially prestigious Catholic prep school in Hackensack, New Jersey. His first year there was a disaster: he quickly became the most unpopular boy at Newman and, in the bargain, did not improve his grades. His second year was better: his literary talents were recognized by his peers and by Father Sigourney Fay, a sophisticated Catholic priest at Newman who introduced him to the Anglo-Irish novelist Shane Leslie and to the American author Henry Adams. Fay and Leslie urged Scott to take pride in his Irish background and were able, for a time, to awaken him to the beauty and spirituality of the Catholic Church.

During his senior year at Newman, Scott decided to apply to Princeton. He was drawn to the university by its air of aristocratic ease and privilege, by its handsome Collegiate Gothic buildings, by its prestigious eating clubs (which he had seen pictures of in *Collier's* magazine), and by the Triangle Club, an undergraduate theatrical group that produced an original musical comedy each fall and sent it on tour over the Christmas holidays. Scott's mother, who had by now inherited her full share of Philip McQuillan's estate, agreed to pay his way, providing he was admitted to the university. He managed to get in by the slimmest of margins, overcoming an unimpressive performance on the entrance exams with some special pleading before the admissions committee. He began at Princeton as a freshman in the fall of 1913.

Scott's academic shortcomings persisted. He was a poor student in college, refusing to study anything that did not engage his imagination and taking the maximum number of class cuts each semester. He was able to stay in school, but only barely. As one of his St. Paul friends put it, "Scott was on the ragged edge of being tolerated academically." Most of his energies went into the Triangle shows, for which he wrote the lyrics, and into close analysis of the Princeton social system, which centered around the eating clubs. These clubs occupied large, handsome buildings on Prospect Avenue and more or less took the place of fraternities, which were not allowed at the university. Scott had set his cap for Cottage, one of the four oldest and most prestigious clubs. (The other three were Ivy, Tiger Inn, and Cap and Gown.) He would receive his bid to Cottage in March 1915, three months after he met Ginevra.

Scott as a teenager at Newman School.

Scott, like Ginevra, was exceptionally good-looking. He was of average size, about five feet seven inches and 160 pounds. He had a trim build and was light on his feet on the dance floor. His blond hair was parted in the middle and carefully combed back; he had a sensitive mouth and a handsome profile. He had developed a good "line"—an amusing, flattering way of talking to a girl that convinced her of his undivided interest. He was skilled in the kind of repartee that passes for conversation among teenagers, and he knew how to draw attention to himself. He was also a fledgling writer: at a dance or a party he might be absorbed in the moment, enjoying the music and color and chatter, but simultaneously he was observing and analyzing, taking mental notes on what created social success and how the pecking order was established within the group. Scott Fitzgerald was an attractive young man who gave most people an impression of ingenuousness and spontaneity. In truth, much of his behavior was studied—calculated for effect and intended to provoke a reaction, usually from the girl he was with.

CHAPTER TWO

The Romance

❧❦❧

Scott met Ginevra in St. Paul on the evening of Monday, January 4, 1915. She was in the city to visit Marie ("Bug") Hersey, a classmate at Westover who had been one of Scott's childhood sweethearts. Ginevra was sixteen years old; Scott, then eighteen, was midway through his second year at Princeton. The two met at an informal party at Marie's house on Summit Avenue. Scott was scheduled to take the Pullman east that night; his Christmas vacation was over, and he was due back at Princeton for classes. He was so smitten with Ginevra, however, that he decided to postpone the journey for twenty-four hours. He wanted to spend Tuesday afternoon with her and to attend a dance being given in her honor Tuesday evening by Elizabeth ("Lib") McDavitt, another local girl. Ginevra was flattered: "Scott perfectly darling," she wrote in her diary that night. "Am dipped about."*

---

* The diaries are original documents in Ginevra's hand and are quoted verbatim. The letters are transcriptions by a typist: obvious errors have been corrected and a few marks of punctuation added for readability.

JANUARY 4

19123

Saturday - rested & went to C.S. for
supper for dancing class. Mou
d.d Dau. was my partner. We
had loads of fun.

Monday. Arrived at St. Paul
at 7.20. Edward met us at the
train and we went to 47? Summit
aus. for breakfast. Saw Hamilton
& Jack & Mrs. Hersey. Had a
bath after breakfast and later on
a shampoo downtown. Went to
Smiths etc. Home for lunch After
lunch - Reuben Warner, Bob Dunn,
Perry Elair + Frank Hurley + I went
to the Orpheum. Awfully funny.
Came home in R's car. Adorable (both)
Dressed for dinner. Perry, Beth, Mudge
Kit Mary; Frank H. Scott Fitz Gerald.
Reuban Jimmie Johnston, Bobbie Schennies
Bill Sindeke - Sat between Scott + Reuben
Danced for a while afterwards Scott
perfectly darling. Am dippied about

They spent the afternoon of January 5th crowded next to each other in the back seat of Reuben Warner's car. (Reuben, a rival for Ginevra's affections, was taking some teenagers for an auto ride across the river to see Minneapolis.) They were together again that evening at Lib McDavitt's dance: this time, however, Scott had to

The place cards from Elizabeth McDavitt's party, preserved by Scott in his scrapbook.

catch his train. He had hoped for time alone with Ginevra at the dance, but he was unable to pry her away from the other party guests. At eleven o'clock he stood with her in the front hall of the McDavitt house. They squeezed hands and exchanged regretful glances; he promised to write, and she promised to answer. The next day she set down her impressions of the party in her diary. "Danced and sat with Scott most all evening," she wrote. "He left for Princeton at 11—oh—!"

On his way back to college, Scott sent this telegram to Ginevra: "PARDON ME IF MY HAND IS A LITTLE SHAKEY BUT I WRITE A VERY SHAKY HAND. I HAVE JUST HAD A QUART OF SAUTERNE AND 3 BRONXES IN CELEBRATION OF MEETING MR. DONAHOE A CLASSMATE OF MINE ON THE TRAIN." As soon as he was back at Princeton, he sent her a special-delivery letter. It was the custom then that if one met a young woman and meant to pursue her seriously, one sent her a "special-

Will Give Bob Party And Supper Tonight For Guest

Miss Elizabeth McDavitt to Entertain for Miss Genevera King of Chicago, House Guest of Miss Marie Hersey.

IN HONOR of Miss Genevera King of Chicago, who is the house guest of Miss Marie Hersey, 475 Summit avenue, Miss Elizabeth McDavitt, 596 Grand avenue, will give a bob party this evening followed by a supper at the home of Miss McDavitt. Among the guests will be the Misses Alida Bigelow, Katherine Ordway, Marie Hersey, Mary Johnston, Grace Warner, Betty Mudge, Constance James, Betty Foster, Eleanor Alair, Mary Butler and Joanne Orten; Messrs. Vernon Rinehart, Frank Hurley, Reuben Warner, Jr., Gustave Schurmeier, Lawrence Boardman, William Lindeke, Robert Barton, James Armstrong, Jr., James Porterfield, Robert Dunn, Scott Fitzgerald, Harrison Johnston.

A newspaper clip describing Lib McDavitt's party, from Scott's scrapbook.

dellie" almost immediately after the first encounter. The letter reached Ginevra on Thursday, January 7th, while she was still visiting in St. Paul. She made a matter-of-fact note of its arrival in her diary: "Got a Special Delivery from *Scott* this morning."

As a popular girl, pursued by many boys, Ginevra might have

expected to receive Scott's special delivery as a matter of course, but she surely did not anticipate the deluge of mail that would follow. Letters began to arrive from her Princeton admirer frequently and

Ginevra's diary for January 5, the day of the party. Scott left at eleven to catch the train east.

in bulk, and her diary entries became more intense with each letter. She received "a *sweet* one from Scott" on January 14th. Another arrived on the fifteenth: "Wonderful letter from Scott again to-day!"

she notes in surprise. On January 23rd: "*Wonderful one from Scott* (he is so darling)." And on January 28th: "*Long wonderful* letter from Scott this morn." On February 6th there arrived a "marvelous wonderful heavenly letter from *Scott*—24 pages—cheered me up immensely." And on February 12th, "*24* pages from Scott. *Thrills.*"

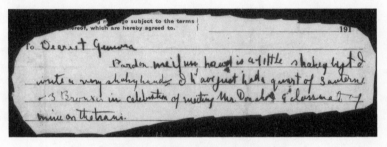

Scott's draft of the telegram he sent to Ginevra
en route from St. Paul to Princeton.

Her affections, she wrote him on February 7th, were "thriving under the stimulus of so much mail."

The dynamics of letter-writing for teenagers of Scott and Ginevra's time were elaborate. A girl's popularity was measured in part by which boys wrote to her and how many letters she received. There was much banter about who was writing to whom and how often the letters were arriving. Many weekday evenings were taken up with letter-writing; popular girls learned to complain about how many boys they had to correspond with. Girls would wander in and out of one another's rooms during letter-writing sessions. One girl might look over another's shoulder as she wrote and, if she knew the boy, might pick up a pen and (with permission) add marginalia or a postscript.

Girls would give readings to their friends from letters they had received; often the girl would supply running commentary on the boy who had written the letter. Certain parts of the letters (the affectionate or intimate bits) would be omitted, although if the boy had been fresh or the girl had a perverse streak, these passages might be read aloud and giggled over. The boys who wrote the letters were aware that this might happen, and they knew to be careful about what they put in their letters. Girls knew it too: boys would show letters to their friends as trophies or would read the sentimental passages aloud—to the accompaniment of eye-rolling and guffaws. No girl wanted to have her personal feelings exposed in this way. Thus there was wariness on both sides until a boy and a girl felt they could trust each other. Only then would they begin to include confidences or confessions of emotion in their letters.

Ginevra does not seem to have worried overly much about this sort of thing. Once she was sure of Scott's interest, she came to enjoy writing to him. "You know, it's queer, but I've always been able to write reams to you and never get bored or tired," she told him on October 13th. He might have said the same thing. So lengthy were his epistles to her that he sometimes had to send them in two envelopes, marked "Part I" and "Part II."

Letter-writing provided Ginevra with an escape. She was not happy about going back to Westover; she made this clear to Scott in her first letter, written on January 11th. "I dread school," she said. "I simply cant go back. I loathe the thought. I curse the fates that call for my education. I rebel at another 8 weeks of grind." Her days at Westover consisted mostly of classes, tests, gym period, glee club, and Bible study (which she began to skip in order to write letters to Scott). Nights were taken up with studying, card games, and chitchat with girlfriends. Incoming letters were the most exciting events of the day.

Most of these missives, one imagines, were pedestrian; boys in their teens typically do not excel at the epistolary arts. Scott Fitzgerald, however, quickly proved himself to be a wonderful correspondent. He was observant and witty, gossipy and funny, full of news and speculations and questions. In other letters of his that have survived from this period, he often included impromptu verse or humorous drawings, and sometimes he sent letter/collages, with cut-out images of swimsuit queens or of movie stars with bobbed hair. Best of all, he could strike a note of longing when he needed to, telling a girl that he was perishing to see her. He must have been a most satisfying young man with whom to trade mail. Ginevra told him so: "Your last letter was a marvel—" she wrote him on January 25th. "I howled over it and wept over it by turns!"

Scott's letters to Ginevra seem to have been playful at first. His opening letter to her (according to her January 11th reply) was signed "Temporarily Devotedly Yrs." She was amused and responded in kind, closing her first letter to him, "Yours *Fickely* sometimes but Devotedly at present. . . ." In the same letter she asked for a photograph of him, claiming to remember only his "yellow hair and big blue eyes." Photographs were an important part of this game and often became objects of near-fetishistic devotion. At one point Ginevra had five photos of Scott on her dresser and another on her desk.

Scott was undoubtedly fascinated with Ginevra, or at least with the image of her that he was carrying about in his head. He continued to write, and she referred to his letters in her replies, sometimes quoting snippets from them. He knew how to keep the correspondence going. He seems to have rationed the flattery, which Ginevra would have been accustomed to, and to have been irreverent instead.

In one letter he asked her how much the Big Four weighed (in toto). In another he sent her a list of current undergraduate slang at Princeton. Later he sent his nominations for an "All-American Petting Team."

Transcript of the first page of Ginevra's opening letter to Scott.

In more serious moments he began to urge Ginevra to reveal herself to him, frankly and honestly. This was a lifelong habit with him. He often questioned people about themselves and prodded them into confessing things that they might not ordinarily have admitted to. Later in his life he irritated some of his friends, including Sara Murphy and Ernest Hemingway, with these interrogations. Ginevra did not reveal much to Scott at first; self-analysis did not come naturally to her. Scott, however, was persistent and pressed her to disclose her techniques. How did she charm so many boys

- 2 -

that I use was undoubtedly " for the love of the trees" not very poetic or original, I assure you.

Scott, what an amazing way you ended your letter ! It was the most characteristic thing I've heard in a long time " Temporarily Devotedly Yrs." Is it still ? I wonder -

I dresd school - I simply cant go back. I loathe the thought. I curse the fates that call for my education. I rebel at another 8 weeks of grind.

Enough of this though, you've probably gone to sleep - Do write me in the future and dont judge my sanity by this letter - oh how the train jolts ---- !

Yours <u>Fickely</u> sometimes but
Devotedly at present -

Ginevra

P. S. The underlined word is supposed to be " fickle"

The second page, Ginevra to Scott, January 11, 1915.

and entice them into falling for her? Ginevra seems to have been puzzled by the question. Scott was assuming that her behavior, like his, was planned for effect. She could not really tell him why so many boys were drawn to her—only that they were, and that she liked the attention. Thus when he called her a vamp in a letter written late in January, she took exception. "I want you to apologize for calling me a vampire," she admonished him on January 29th. "Très rude I should say."

Ginevra did reveal a little about herself in her letters: "I *know* I am a flirt and I can't stop it," she admitted on January 20th. "A few years ago I took pleasure in being called 'fast,' " she confessed; "I didn't care *how* I acted, I liked it, and so I didn't care for what people said." But that attitude had not lasted: "About a year ago I began to see that there was something better in life than what I had been doing, and I honestly tried to act properly, but I am afraid I'll never be able to wholly reform." She understood the double standard of her time: "I am pretty good on the whole, but you know how much alike we are, and in a boy it doesn't matter, but a girl has to control her feelings, which *is* hard for me, as I am emotional." These confidences, she hoped, were what he was after. "This is the kind of letter you said you wanted," she told him, "and so this is what I wrote."

Scott soon learned that his romance with Ginevra was causing a stir at Westover. On February 6th he received a cryptic telegram telling him not to expect his usual letter from her the following day. "G.K.'S DAILY DELAYED. UNAVOIDABLE. REASON EXPLAINED LATER," read the wire. A special delivery from Ginevra arrived the next day to explain what had happened. One of her friends from down the hall had wandered into her room while she was composing a letter to him. The girl had wanted to read the letter, but Ginevra had refused to show it to her. The girl had tried to snatch it, precipitating a playful tussle. "In the scramble I shut up the letter in the desk-drawer, and it went *so* tight that no amount of pulling would open it," she explained. "I only had 15 minutes to get it in the last mail . . . and we got started laughing and then of course lost all our strength—I was screaming— So Midge said—'Well, it's my fault, now I'll send a telegram and tell him he wont get his daily letter.' . . . I said all right, so she went and did it." This was heady stuff for an eighteen-year-old college boy. He was becoming, in absentia, a celebrity at Westover.

Scott at Princeton, 1916.

Ginevra knew how to provoke Scott. In a January 25th letter she recalled their farewell in St. Paul and his failure to kiss her. "I hear you had plans for kissing me goodbye publicly," she wrote him. "My goodness, I'm glad you didn't— I'd have had to be severe as anything with you!" Though perhaps not, to judge from her next sentence: "*Ans. this— Why didn't you?* (KISS ME)."

One of Scott's photos of Ginevra, preserved in his scrapbook.

Ginevra began to dream about Scott. She slept with his letters (a mildly erotic detail), hoping that dreams about him would come in the night. At first she refused to tell him about the dreams, only that in one of them he had done "the rescuing act." But in a February 8th letter she relented and told him about one dream: "Last night I dreamt you were calling on me," she wrote, "only you had purple hair, and would insist upon strutting around and tapping on all the walls, saying 'Even walls have ears.' " Probably Scott had hoped for something more romantic, though this particular dream suggests that Ginevra had already noticed a certain mistrustfulness in his nature. In several of his letters (to judge from her answers) he told her not to let others read what he had written. This prohibition disappointed her, and she eventually said so in a letter of April 4th:

> I'll tell you the honest truth. Your letters are so wonderful and so amusing that it seems a shame that some of the poor letter-less females who have a sense of humour up here shouldn't be *read* some of the funny parts of some of your letters. But really and truly and honestly, Scott, I wouldn't for the world show any of the really "nice" parts, because other people would think them foolish and would also think that I was a nut to let you string me along with what they thought was bull.

FITZGERALD DECIDED to visit Ginevra at Westover. They had been together for only a few hours in St. Paul, and he wanted very much to see her again. She felt the same: "I would simply *adore* to have you come," she wrote him on January 29th. There were complications, however. "The difficulty," she explained, "is that you can only come on Saturdays—from four till six." Visits were carefully supervised: "The worst thing," she warned him, "is that you must sit in a glass case." Ginevra meant that the girls could only entertain boys in drawing rooms that had large glass doors. The young people were observed during these visits by chaperones who sat nearby; certainly no kissing was permitted, though some clandestine hand-holding might be managed. Further, the girls were forbidden to wear cosmetics and had to dress in their school uniforms. "When you see us appearing in simple white 'girlish' frocks, dont fall over backwards," she told him five days before he came.

Scott made the visit on Saturday, February 20th, accompanied by a classmate named Joe Shanley, who also had a girl at Westover. It was a considerable trek for the two boys; they had to take the spur line from Princeton to Princeton Junction and catch a train from there to Penn Station in New York. They walked to Grand Central, took a local train to Waterbury, and rode a trolley out to Westover. They arrived a half-hour late. Scott, though he had been warned about the visiting rules, was disappointed that he could not be alone with Ginevra. She, however, was more than satisfied. That night she wrote down her feelings in her diary:

Scott came in afternoon

Oh it was so wonderful to see him again. I am madly in love with him. He is so wonderful—Came up from Princeton with Joe Shanley. . . . Marvelous time.

Early in their correspondence Scott revealed his jealous side, questioning her about her other beaux, including Reuben Warner, the rival from St. Paul, and Deering Davis, a Chicago boy who, according to Ginevra's diary, was a "divine dancer." Ginevra's letters back were full of reassurances: "Scott, why *wont* you believe what I said about your standing first—" she wrote him on February 8th. "I can't tell you any better or any more truthfully, and I wouldn't have told you at all, if you hadn't asked me plainly. Really Scott, there's nothing in the world I was ever more sincere about—! Believe me or not!"

He did believe her, but then again he didn't. He tried to awaken her jealousies by deliberately putting another girl's name on the envelope of one of his letters, then crossing it out and substituting Ginevra's name and address. Ginevra took it in stride: she wasn't fooled, though from time to time she did suspect him of inconstancy. "I have a feeling that you're keeping something from me—"

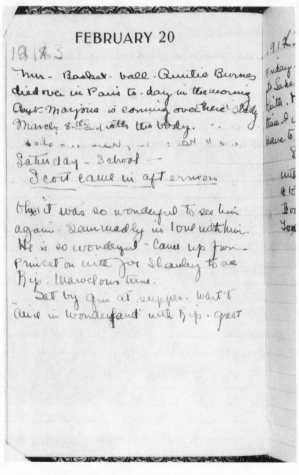

The diary entry for the day Scott visited Ginevra at Westover.

she wrote him on March 10th. "Villain—Enclose (Unclose it, I mean) Hidden heart affair, I'll bet— You might tell me, Scott. I might give the other party advice. . . ."

From time to time in her letters Ginevra breaks into French, a language that Scott was studying at Princeton. Her efforts are commendably good, though now and then she resorts to Franglais: "See? Comprenez— Understandez-vous?" In the same letter, dated March 12th, she complains about a small accident: "I ran a wet pen up my finger yesterday and it has gotten infected so I cant write a word with this bulky old bandage on. I know I'm going to die of blood poisoning. Wilt come to mine funeral—? Say Yea—and bring a nosegay of dandy lions— Ah, I die content—! For I shall die, I shall die—I shall jolly well die D-I-E die———die———die—! Amen."

By now Scott had fallen into the habit of analyzing Ginevra's personality in his letters to her. At first she seems to have been intrigued by his diagnoses, but soon she began to find them irritating. "Dont you fool yourself," she told him on February 25th; "you haven't got me 'catalogued' yet." Still they continued to write, and Ginevra was proud of her ability to match him page for page. "In six weeks I used up a ream of paper," she told him on March 8th, "and to be perfectly truthful, most of it was on you." She saved his letters: "I wouldn't throw yours away for the world," she assured him on April 19th. She had them "locked up in my strong-box—only there are so many that they dont all quite go in!"

Throughout Ginevra's letters one finds frequent notes of longing and frustration. She and Scott cannot see each other; they have only letters and photographs. On March 12th, her emotions spill over: "Oh Scott," she writes, "*why* aren't we——————— somewhere else to-night. Why aren't we at a dance in summer now with a full moon a big lovely garden and soft music in the distance." For the first time she signs the letter "Love, Ginevra." Surely Scott read this letter over more than once. Perhaps he wondered about the long, tantalizing dash. What might she have wanted to say?

Scott kept this photograph of Ginevra in his watch case.

In mid-March, Ginevra went home for spring vacation. She was happy to escape from school: "Away from the damned old hole—!" she wrote in her diary on the sixteenth. Her parents had moved into their new house on Astor Street, and she was delighted by its beauty and luxury. These visits home were treats: according to her diary she slept late, had breakfast in bed, went shopping for new clothes, and had lunch downtown at the Blackstone Hotel. Scott was unable to visit her, but this did not curtail her social activities. In her letters to him (when she had time to write) she reported a whirl of parties and dances, with much attention from other boys.

His suspicions returned: sometime late in March he wrote her, "Even now you may be having a tete-a-tete with some 'unknown Chicagoan' with crisp dark hair and glittering smile." Ginevra quoted the accusatory sentence in her March 25th reply, then indulged in a little goading. "You needn't worry about me," she wrote. "Of course you think that because I'm here with a lot of boys, I have forgotten you, but I know it'll make me like you all the better, because you see, all last term I didn't think of a thing but *you*—(this is as sincere as I've *ever* been) and by the end of the term naturally my mental powers had given out." Then she added, maddeningly, "There are some peachy boys here now."

Fitzgerald seems to have told Ginevra in one of his letters that she was emotionally shallow. This angered her and prompted her, in the same March 25th letter, to deliver a short homily on the subject of love. "I know you cant mistake true love—I *know* it," she wrote him. "And it's a sin not to recognize it." She stood up for herself: "I defy you, Scott Fitzgerald! I have love in me. . . . You show your ignorance of my nature well by saying that I haven't ever really *loved* anybody. *Naturally* I'm awfully, awfully young, but there have been times in my life, in the last few years, where I felt something deeper and truer and more sincere than mere shallow affection. You see, I've done a lot more for my age than almost any girl. . . ."

Fitzgerald, perhaps chastened, invited her to the Sophomore Prom—the most important social event of the year at Princeton for members of his class. She was excited: "Scott—*I must see you!!*" she wrote on March 26th. Again, though, there was an obstacle. A girl of Ginevra's age and social position had to be chaperoned on such occasions, usually by her mother. Mrs. King, after some delay, told her daughter that she could not come east for the prom, and Ginevra, regretfully, had to turn down Scott's invitation. "I'm so disap. about the dance I cant see straight," she wrote him on April 26th. By way of compensation, Mrs. King did journey east in early June to bring Ginevra home for the summer, and Scott was allowed to meet the two women in Manhattan on June 8th and to be

Ginevra's escort for the evening. Ginevra recorded the events of the entire day (which began at her school) in the diary:

> Up at 5.00—New York at ten. Ma met me and we shopped *hard* all day. *Scott* came for dinner which we had on the Ritz roof garden. . . . "Nobody Home" afterwards. Then to Ziefield's Midnight Frolic at New Amsterdam. Bed at *1*—

The entry needs a little explaining. *Nobody Home* was a popular play that was running at the Princess Theater; Ginevra's father had bought the tickets for them during a recent trip to New York. *The Midnight Frolic,* a show produced by the theater impresario Florenz Ziegfeld, whose name Ginevra misspells, was a gaudy, leggy affair presented nightly in the roof garden atop the New Amsterdam Theater on West 42nd Street. Scott never forgot the evening. He remembered it years later in his essay "My Lost City," where he recalled the night Ginevra "made luminous the Ritz Roof on a brief passage through."

Scott managed to visit Ginevra in Lake Forest later that same month. He was on his way to Montana, where he would spend part of his summer vacation on the family ranch of a school friend. Ginevra and her mother were headed in the opposite direction, to Biddeford Pool, a fashionable resort in Maine. "We see each other so little that it is funny," wrote Ginevra on August 2nd. "Why couldn't we have chosen places nearer to each other?" Ginevra did a little calculation and sent it to Scott on August 25th: "I told you, didn't I, that I figured out that we have seen each other for exactly *15* hours."

It's possible, of course, that Scott preferred things this way. On the few occasions when he and Ginevra had actually been together, she had been in her element and completely in control. She was invariably the center of attention, while he was only another of the many boys who were pursuing her. When he had visited her in Lake Forest in June he had probably hoped for special treatment—some recognition that he was her top man, perhaps, and a little time alone with her so that he might pursue the elusive kiss. But she was so busy

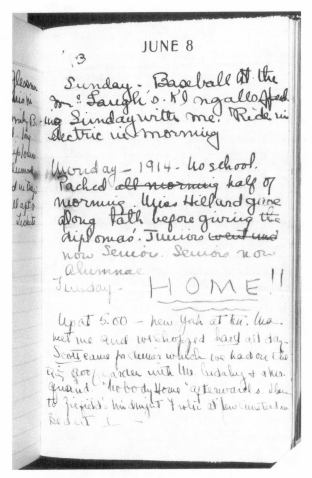

The magical evening with Scott on the roof garden of the Ritz; then home for the summer.

and popular, so much in demand, that he could not get close. She would not dismiss the other boys and grant him the audience alone that he craved.

Furthermore, he was not on firm ground in Lake Forest. He was of Irish descent and was a Roman Catholic, both of which were disadvantages there. Most of the boys in Ginevra's social set were backed by high social status and family money. Their fathers were railroad executives or lumber barons or department-store magnates or prominent physicians, attorneys, or judges. Scott's father was a wholesale grocery salesman, and not an especially successful one. Scott did have good looks, charm, and literary ability, but these were not the trump cards. His visits to Lake Forest must have been difficult for him. In the field of letter-writing, however, he was unrivaled. Here he shone, and he knew it. At his desk, composing a letter to Ginevra, there were no competitors hanging about in the stag line, nor was there anyone to remind him that he was a young man of modest means, hobnobbing with the rich.

CHAPTER THREE

Ginevra's Story

᠅

Ginevra and Scott kept up their letter-writing that summer, but the tone of the correspondence began to change. Her letters (one of which begins "Dear Fitz—" and another of which is signed "Fraternally yours") are less frequent and not as affectionate. "For *heaven's sake DONT* idealize me!" she had warned him earlier, on May 14th, perhaps in an attempt to cool his ardor. "You're so darling and I wish I could see you again as you're so nice and I'd like to talk to you," she added. "You sound as though you had given up hope of kissing me within a year and a half—!" These were surely not the sentiments that Scott wanted to see in her letters.

Ginevra wrote almost nothing about Scott in her diary that summer. It's possible that, having seen him against the social backdrop of Lake Forest, as opposed to St. Paul or Westover, she had realized that she should probably not encourage him as a suitor. She would turn seventeen in November; if all went according to custom, she would become a debutante at eighteen. Engagement and marriage often followed quickly after the debut for young women of her social class. Scott Fitzgerald, though handsome and clever, was not a matrimonial possibility. He and she saw each other in New Haven at the Yale-Princeton football game in November 1915, but that was their only encounter that fall. Ginevra's subsequent letters began to sound more mature: "Acting like a fool isn't the only interesting thing to do in this world," she wrote him on January 27th.

Fitzgerald began to pick quarrels with Ginevra in his letters. He seems to have doubted her loyalty to him and to have been suspicious about her romances with other boys. She was quite open with him on this score, mentioning the names of the young men she liked and telling him about the parties and dances she was escorted to. Some of Scott's anger was probably staged. He would write her an angry letter and then (to judge from her reply) take it all back in the next letter. Ginevra recognized this behavior for what it was and refused to react. At first her responses were reassuring and conciliatory; later, near the end of the romance, she became weary of the charade.

Fitzgerald had other and more important reasons to be upset in the fall and winter of 1915–16. His desultory study habits at Princeton had put him into serious academic trouble. He had continued to cut classes and to accumulate "conditions"—failing grades, especially in math, which he had to work off by tutoring and extra exams. In December 1915 he acknowledged temporary defeat and dropped out of Princeton for the rest of the academic year. He claimed that he was developing a tubercular condition, which might have been true, and returned to St. Paul to live at home during the spring semester.

He and his friend Edmund Wilson, the future literary critic, had written the Triangle show for that fall, a farce called *The Evil Eye*. The academic authorities at Princeton, however, had forbidden

Fitzgerald to act in the show or to go along on its holiday tour because of his low grades and poor health. In January 1916, *The Evil Eye* played in Chicago for two performances. Scott was not allowed to attend. Ginevra, however, went to both shows and sent this report to him on January 17th:

> I just had to write you and tell you how perfectly divine I thought the whole Princeton Triangle show and people were! Why Scott, it was the most marvelous thing I have

Scott's Triangle Club watch charm, which he gave to Ginevra.
She returned it to Scott's daughter, Scottie, in 1950;
today it is worn by Scott's great-granddaughter,
Blake Hazard, on a charm bracelet.

> ever known. I sat in the front row for both performances, and was crazier than ever about it the second time. While [the boys in the show] were in Chicago I went to a luncheon for them, and was practically the only girl that wasn't a debutante! Sat by Sam Cooper. . . . [He] said that he imagined me a peroxide blond, of the chorus-girl type— My Lord, Scott, what had you been telling him?

A review in the Princeton student newspaper, the *Daily Princetonian*, gave this account of the Chicago performance: "Three hundred young ladies occupied the front rows of the house and, following the show, they stood up, gave the Princeton locomotive and tossed their bouquets at the cast and chorus." One of those young ladies

The cast photo for The Evil Eye, *the 1916 Triangle Club show written by Scott and his friend Edmund Wilson.*

was Ginevra King. The songs that she and her friends were cheering were Scott's creations, as were many other features of the production. His name appeared with Wilson's on the title page of the programme. It would have been a considerable triumph for him to have been there with Ginevra on his arm, chatting with her Lake Forest friends during the intermissions and accepting their compliments. Instead he was stuck at home, drifting, grounded by low grades and bad health.

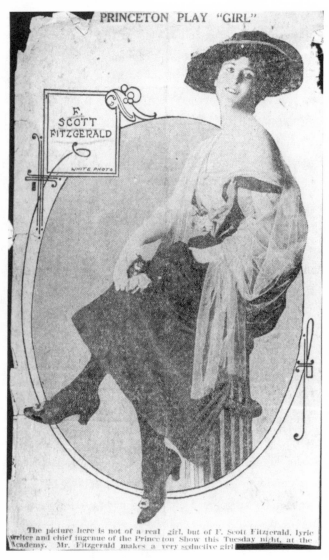

F.
SCOTT
FITZGERALD

WHITE PHOTO

The picture here is not of a real girl, but of F. Scott Fitzgerald, lyric writer and chief ingenue of the Princeton Show this Tuesday night, at the Academy. Mr. Fitzgerald makes a very seductive girl

Scott in drag, advertising The Evil Eye.

In May 1916, Ginevra faced a crisis of her own. She and two of her classmates broke the school rules at Westover by leaning out of their dormitory windows and talking to several boys who were there for the senior dance. This bit of impulsiveness sounds relatively innocent, but Miss Hillard did not think so. She summoned Ginevra and the two other girls into her office and, according to Ginevra's account in a May 22nd letter, called them "bold, bad hussies" and "adventuresses." Their explanations were "honeycombed with deceit," and their "honour was stained." Miss Hillard told the girls that they must leave Westover immediately after exams, though she rescinded this punishment when she learned that several other girls had also been talking to boys from their windows.

Ginevra telephoned her father, who was in New York on business, and he came out to Westover. To judge by the account in the May 22nd letter to Scott, the meeting between Charles King and Miss Hillard did not go well:

> Mind you, after all the things that demon had told me, she was as sweet as sugar to Father, even if he did tell her a few plain truths about herself— You wouldn't have known her for the same woman. She was all smiles, and agreed heartily when Father said he thought the best thing to do would be to take me home, and she was sweet as anything to me when I said "goodbye" to her. . . . So I left last Monday morn and since then Pa has gotten a letter flattering me to the skies, and Father answered her by ripping her clean up the back. . . . We haven't heard anything from that yet—

Miss Hillard offered to reinstate Ginevra with no penalties, but Charles King would not hear of it. He withdrew his daughter from

Westover and enrolled her for the coming fall in a finishing school in Manhattan—Miss McFee's on West 72nd Street. Ginevra had in fact been thinking of going elsewhere for her senior year, but she had made close friends at Westover and had enjoyed some fun outside of classes. Now these memories would be tainted. She never

The three women who ran Westover School.
Left to right: Mary Hillard (the headmistress),
Helen La Monte, Lucy Pratt.

forgot her "firing" from Westover, nor did she ever entirely forgive Miss Hillard.

GINEVRA'S DEPARTURE from Westover took place in May 1916, but her romantic disengagement from Scott began earlier. Perhaps he sensed this and allowed his budding authorial instincts to take over. Living at home in the early months of 1916, with little else to occupy his time, he wrote two stories about himself and Ginevra and sent her the manuscripts. These stories were his initial efforts to capture their romance in fiction.*

The first narrative was called "The Perfect Hour," a title which Scott took from Ginevra. The notion of "the perfect hour" had been running through her letters to him: what would it be like, she had wondered, if the two of them could be truly alone for one perfect hour? What if there were no glass-enclosed parlors or bothersome chaperones or curious parents or desirous suitors or Lake Forest friends or loud football crowds? Would their feelings for each other reawaken? "Honestly and truly," Ginevra had written him on January 31st, "it would be wonderful to have that perfect hour, sometime, someday and somewhere." But they never did. Scott, by now, must have realized that such perfect moments only exist in fiction. He therefore wrote "The Perfect Hour" and mailed it to her in February; she was charmed by the story and read it aloud to one of her suitors, who pronounced it "divine."

Scott's effort inspired Ginevra to produce a story of her own. She sent it to him, without a title, on March 6th. "Enclosed you'll find out my idea of what a 'Perfect Hour' is," she wrote him, "so you see my idea is quite different from yours." Ginevra's story is printed on the pages that follow. While reading it, one should keep in mind that it was written by the seventeen-year-old girl who would one day be the principal model for Daisy Buchanan in *The Great Gatsby.*

---

* Neither manuscript has survived; both presumably perished when Ginevra destroyed Scott's letters to her.

[Ginevra's Story]

...

The wedding-bells were gayly chiming and all the inhabi-
tants of the town were excited, as to-day Ginevra King was
to wed the Count Spagettioni. Everyone expected it to be
one of the prettiest weddings of the season, and were proud
of the Chicago girl who had been won by a titled Russian—

At quarter after two there was a final rustle of excitement;
heads and necks were craned towards the door, which finally
died away in an excited hush, broken at last by the triumphal
and immortal strains of Lohengrin's Wedding March—

————*The ceremony was on*————*!!!*—

With a passionate gesture she flung off the crimson scarf that
wrapped in glowing folds her slim form. In her eyes there
lurked a subtle transient indefinite look that contrasted
drolly with her fine aristocratic face. Her lips were pressed in
an angry line, and her brow was darkened by a deep scowl.

How—*How* could it be accomplished? For days—
months—years—centuries, it seemed she had been living—
breathing under a false atmosphere. Leonardo was good but no,
he could not give her what she craved—affection—*real deep*
sympathy. He gave her all he could in his reserved, unsympa-
thizing way and she was thankful of the fact that he adored her.
But an indefinable something was lacking in her married life—
and that thing (if she could have guessed it) was *L O V E!*

Seated on a large divan, her head in her jewelled hands and buried in deep thought, the half-hours sped by till finally as the tiny diamond encrusted clock on the console struck five, she started up suddenly, and with an excited motion, gazed wildly at herself in the mirror—

"Ginevra—you're dreaming—*no* it *can't* be *you*! Would you—*could* you dare! But where—where would you go!"

Again her gaze shifted to a tiny little locket on her arm. In a flash, she opened it, and gazed at the picture with-in.

With a decisive nod she grasped her crimson veil from the bronze, and ran out [of] the room, up the broad marble stairs, and into her dainty boudoir. Twenty minutes after she was walking out the front door, clad in an elaborate street costume and muffled beyond recognition in her voluptuous blue fox furs.

Her "Rolls-Royce" was waiting and for the next ten minutes she was speeding past the beautiful residences of the popular suburb, to the cozy station, just catching the last train for the city.—

※

The clock was striking ten when she turned down a side street, and walked through a small court, into the vestibule of a fashionable apartment [building].

"Mr. Fitz-Gerald's apartment, please," she inquired of the elevator boy.

"Fo'th flo', ma'am—" as he tore up the shaft madly and deposited her in front of a large mahogany door.

A tall sombre butler answered her summons.

"Mr. Fitz-Gerald at home?"

"Yes'm, step in here a moment, pleas'm—I'll call him!"

The whole apartment was furnished in black and yellow, shading into cream. The marble floor was made up [of] large squares, the wall panelling cream, and with black hangings. A large concert grand stood in one corner littered with operatic scores. A huge silver picture frame showed Melba in "Carmen" and Mary Pickford in "A Good Little Devil."[*] Hanging in an alcove was a large painting, beautifully lighted and framed with decorative yellow and black banners of Mr. Fitz-Gerald, "most beautiful of show girls."[†] Tapestries of "Old Nassau" hung everywhere, and the andirons in the fireplace were in the form of tigers. In front of this fireplace, now bright and blazing, and casting lurid yellow streaks over the unique room was a large comfortable Morris chair, of black leather. It was by far the most comfortable spot in the room, and was undoubtedly Mr. Fitz-Gerald's palladium.

The Countess picked up a "Princeton Tiger" and was turning over the leaves when a cheery whistle came from the recesses of the abode—"Beware—of—the—Evil—Eye—"

and Mr. Fitz-Gerald strode into the room.

The Countess gave a start. She would scarcely have recognized in this man her friend of former years. His handsome stern face showed few traces of boyhood. Around his

---

[*] Nellie Melba was a mezzo-soprano famous for her performances in Bizet's *Carmen*. Mary Pickford played Juliet (a fairy) in *A Good Little Devil*, a play that ran on Broadway during the winter and spring of 1913. Ginevra probably saw her repeat the role in the 1914 silent-film version of the play.

[†] Ginevra has in mind the photograph of Fitzgerald dressed in drag, taken to publicize *The Evil Eye*. The photo is reproduced on p. 47 of this book.

mouth was a determined yet melancholy look and in his eyes was a new light—that of a thriving business man. He was dressed in a brown and white checked suit which suited his thin sun-burned face.

Upon perceiving the Countess reading the "Tiger" he smiled.

"Very well edited—that. Used to run it myself—a few years ago—y'know!"

After this remark the Countess felt more at her ease.

"Well—?" interrogatively—

"I don't suppose you know who I am," she started in a hurt tone.

"Let me see—Did you apply for that position in my last moving picture? It *was* you, wasn't it?"

The Countess was horrified. "Indeed no,—I—well, do you remember the name Ginevra?"

"Ginevra?—Ginevra?—Oh yes, that patent tooth paste* they asked me to boost in one of my movies—Yes, yes! It wasn't very good. I advise you—"

"No, oh don't you remember me? I've come all the way from the country to see you!"

"Listen, lady, if you're looking for a job, don't come to me. My places are all full—"

"But—Scott—!!"

"What, calling me Scott? What *do* you want anyway?"

"Do you remember Marie Hersey?"

---

* Perhaps a reference to King's Tooth Powder, produced by Thomsen-King & Co. of Chicago.

"Oh yes, my old friend Bug, yes, yes. I've written several movies about her. So you know her?"

"Well, I've known her all my life—and once—in 1914—I visited her—in St. Paul—at Xmas—and I met you and you wrote me all that winter—and—oh *now* can't you remember me now!" She collapsed in a spasm of tears—

"Good Grief—don't cry—you'd almost do for [my] new opera—'When Tears are Wet.' Who are you anyhow?"

"Ginevra King."

"Ginevra King—just [a] minute—1914—" He ran to the table, opened the drawer and took out a box of files—

"Let me see. Wolcott—Helen, Teale—Ruth, Robertson—Fandria, Sturtevant—Ruth, etc. etc. etc. Ah, here we are. King—Ginevra—Xmas—1914—Short Stocky—dark, fair looker and dancer—passionate—no character—personality—no brains—letters best part (N.B. Look in compartment old letters—For picture—Look file T. 99th from top—Characteristic music—'China Town'—)"*

"Well, well, so I used to know you—how pleasant this is. Sit down and we'll talk over old times. Will you have a little something? Sherry—or perhaps a cocktail? Pardon me a moment!"

The Countess was completely crushed and sat staring unheedingly into the blazing fire. There she saw, vanishing with the last of her beautiful air-castles, the vision of a perfect hour. She—Scott—the quiet dreamy fire—perfect peace, for

* "Chinatown, My Chinatown," with words by William Jerome and music by Jean Schwartz, from the 1910 musical *Up and Down Broadway*. The American Quartet had a number one hit with the song in 1915, recording it with Victor.

an hour only and now this was fading away like a spent rose. She ought to have realized that it could never have come true, and now she must go back to the Count and the old life— a changed woman—without a heart—! Her sense of loss was beyond expression and she shivered as she sat deep in thought. Suddenly she was rudely awakened by F.S.F.'s return with the cocktails—

"Won't you stay a little longer," he said cheerily. "My wife ought to be home directly!"—

FINIS—

There are broad similarities between Ginevra's story and *The Great Gatsby.* Her story, like Fitzgerald's novel, is about a reunion. Her "Ginevra" character, like Daisy Buchanan, is married to a wealthy man with whom she is unhappy. Jewels, furs, and a luxury car have not satisfied her; she wants love and emotional fulfillment. "Ginevra" seeks out an old flame named "Scott Fitz-Gerald"— apparently she has kept up with him and knows where he lives (as Gatsby has kept up with Daisy). "Scott" is now a celebrity, connected in some way with the movie industry and the stage. He lives in elaborately decorated quarters and is looked after by a somber servant. He wears a brown-and-white-checked outfit that might have hung in Jay Gatsby's closet, right next to the famous pink suit. Certain details in the story catch the eye: the clock in the sitting room, for example, brings to mind the clock on the mantel in Nick Carraway's bungalow—an important detail in the reunion scene between Daisy and Gatsby. And the "Wedding March" from

Lohengrin, which Ginevra mentions early in her story, is used to good symbolic effect by Fitzgerald in the Plaza scene in *Gatsby*.

Fitzgerald had Ginevra's letters and her story in his possession throughout his career. Did he reread the story at some point during the composition of *Gatsby* and use it to stimulate his imagination? One doesn't wish to insist on these correspondences too strongly, but it's certainly possible. Fitzgerald began to plan a new novel in the summer of 1922; his initial plan was to set it in the Midwest around the year 1885. According to a June 20, 1922, letter to Maxwell Perkins, his editor at Scribners, the novel was to have "a catholic element." This narrative, however, failed to develop, and by the spring of 1924 Fitzgerald had stopped working on it. He discarded most of the drafts, salvaging only the short story "Absolution," a tale about a dreamy, imaginative boy named Rudolph Miller who tells a lie in confession.

Perhaps at this juncture Fitzgerald, in search of material and inspiration, read back through Ginevra's letters and came upon her story. This was typical of his composing habits: he often read over old documents or letters or searched through his personal ledger for a sentence or a word or an image, something that would stimulate his memories. Ginevra's story would have brought back thoughts of their romance and might have caused him to speculate about what a reunion between a self-made man and a wealthy woman, both of them still young, would be like if placed at the center of a novel.

There are other connections between Fitzgerald's romance with Ginevra and the story he tells in *The Great Gatsby*. Daisy Buchanan resembles Ginevra physically; her voice, full of money, seems to be Ginevra's voice. Daisy is from Louisville, but Tom Buchanan, her polo-playing husband, is (like Charles King, Ginevra's father) a

Ginevra's friend Edith Cummings, the original
for Jordan Baker in The Great Gatsby.

Yale man from Lake Forest. Jordan Baker, Daisy's best friend in the novel, is a version of Edith Cummings, Ginevra's close friend and a member of the Big Four. (Fitzgerald identified Edith as the model for Jordan in a December 20, 1924, letter to Perkins.) Fitzgerald had likely seen Edith Cummings at Westover and at Lake Forest. She was much in the news for her golfing while Fitzgerald was at work on *Gatsby*. She had won the U.S. Women's Amateur title in 1923 and had followed with a victory in the Western Amateur in 1924. Reporters called her the "Fairway Flapper"; her photo appeared on the cover of *Time* magazine on August 25, 1924.

These connections are only suggestive. Other sources for *The Great Gatsby* are more certain: the *Satyricon* of Petronius, for example, and the rigging of the 1919 World Series by Arnold Rothstein. Still, the correspondences between Ginevra's story and Fitzgerald's novel are close enough to suggest that her story might have had an influence, perhaps even an important one, on the genesis of the novel.

The story is important for another reason. It shows that Ginevra, perceptive beyond her years, had realized what Scott had been doing. He had been gathering material—observing her, analyzing her personality, and making mental notes on her world of money, status, and privilege. The card file on old girlfriends that "Scott Fitz-Gerald" has compiled in the story is a clue to Ginevra's thoughts. The real Scott Fitzgerald, she believed, had been sizing her up. If she remained alive in his memory it would be as a model for the female characters he meant one day to create.

CHAPTER FOUR

Endings   and   Beginnings

I n April or May 1916, Scott sent Ginevra another story, this one called "The Ideal Day," in which "Ginevra" entertains "Scott" by playing golf. She was supposed to compose a second story of her own and send it to him, but she never did. "I've got to wait till I feel like writing it," she explained on May 24th, "and that feeling hasn't come yet—!" He saw her in Lake Forest in August; this was the visit during which someone said to him, "Poor boys shouldn't think of marrying rich girls."

The following month Ginevra enrolled at Miss McFee's in New York, an easy train ride away from Princeton. Her letters to Scott, however, suggest that she was not in any particular hurry to visit him. In early October he invited her to come to Princeton for the football game against Yale, but she was not keen to make the trip. She delayed in giving him an answer and dropped hints in an October 15th letter that he might want to invite another girl. "Please ask someone else if you cant wait," she urged. "Be frank and earnest."

Scott was now beginning to write about Ginevra for publication. He told her that he was basing a character on her in a short story that he was writing for the *Nassau Lit,* the campus literary magazine at Princeton. She liked the idea: "It would be slick to have you write a story about me," she told him on November 3rd. He called the story "Babes in the Woods" and eventually published it in the *Nassau Lit* for May 1917. "Babes," which is reprinted as an appendix in this book, is an imaginative re-creation of their first meeting in St. Paul, a skillfully done piece that captures their innocence and their guile.

Fitzgerald's ledger entry for August 1916.
"Poor boys shouldn't think of marrying rich girls."

Ginevra did go to Princeton for the Yale game in November, but by now she had lost interest in Fitzgerald and had, with another girl, made a date to meet two Yale boys in New York after the game. Almost sixty years later, in an interview with a writer from the *Princeton Alumni Weekly,* she told the story of what had happened. Late in the afternoon she and Scott, along with the other girl and her Princeton beau, had taken the train to Penn Station. "My girlfriend and I had made plans to meet some other, uh, friends," she recalled. "So we said good-bye, we were going back to school, thanks so much. Behind the huge pillars in the station there were two guys waiting for us—Yale boys. We couldn't just walk out and leave

"Babes in the Woods"

At the top of the stairs she paused. The emotions of divers on spring boards, leading ladies on opening nights and brawny bestriped young men on the day of the Big Game crowded through her. She felt as if she should have descended to a burst of drums or to a discordant blend of gems from Thais and Carmen. She had never been so worried about her appearance, she had never been so satisfied with it. She had been sixteen years old for two months.

"Isabelle!" called Helêne from her doorway

"I'm ready" she caught a slight lump or nervousness in her throat.

"I've got on the wrong slippers and stockings —— you'll have to wait a minute".

Isabelle started toward Helêne's door for a last peak at a mirror, but something decided her to stand there and gaze down the stairs. They curved tantalizingly and she could just catch a glimpse

Initial page of the manuscript of "Babes in the Woods,"
the first story Scott ever wrote about Ginevra.

them standing behind the pillars. Then we were scared to death we'd run into Scott and his friend. But we didn't. I think they'd just headed for the bar."

The romance ended, according to an entry in Scott's ledger, in January 1917. Later that year, in October, he published a story in the *Nassau Lit* entitled "The Pierian Springs and the Last Straw"; the story suggests that he and Ginevra had a quarrel at one of her school dances in Manhattan. Perhaps this happened, perhaps he made it up. In any case the romance was over by the end of January.

In the months that followed, however, Scott became worried about his letters. Would Ginevra show them to friends and make light of the feelings that he had written into them? These fears were probably not justified, but Scott was emotionally bruised and was troubled about many things, not just the end of his romance with Ginevra. He had continued to perform poorly in the classroom at Princeton and had decided not to pursue a degree further. The United States had entered World War I that spring, and he had enlisted in the army, determined not to miss what he was certain would be the major event of his generation. The war also gave him a semi-honorable exit from the university. Like most of his contemporaries who were signing up, Fitzgerald thought that he might die on a battlefield in Europe; apparently he did not want his letters to Ginevra to survive him. He wrote her about his concerns in late June or early July, and she replied with this billet-doux on July 7, 1917:

> *Dear Scott—*
>
> *I have destroyed your letters—so you needn't be afraid that they will be held up as incriminating evidence. They were harmless—have you a guilty conscience?*

*I'm sorry you think that I would hold them up to you as
I never did think they meant anything.*

If it isn't too much trouble you might destroy mine too.

Sincerely

Ginevra

Fitzgerald spent the war in training camps. He was commis-
sioned as a second lieutenant in October 1917 but didn't "get over"
to the battlefields in France and Belgium. His energies during the
war were spent in writing a novel called *The Romantic Egotist,*
which he composed in officers' clubs during evenings and week-
ends. The manuscript was submitted twice to Scribners, and twice
rejected, but it formed the basis of *This Side of Paradise,* the novel
Scribners eventually did accept for publication.

From October 1917 to May 1918, Scott was stationed in military
camps in Kansas, Kentucky, and Georgia. In June 1918 he was sent
to Camp Sheridan, a military installation near Montgomery, Alabama. There in July he met Zelda Sayre, a seventeen-year-old belle
known locally for her beauty, wit, and daring. Scott was captivated
by Zelda—by her disregard for convention and, as with Ginevra, by
the fact that she was the "top girl" in her social circle. Zelda already
had a reputation as a speed and was pursued by many young men.
For Scott this only added to her allure.

In July 1918, the same month in which he met Zelda, Scott wrote
to Ginevra in Chicago, perhaps in hopes of resuming their correspondence. She sent Scott this reply on July 15th:

Dear Scott:—

*I certainly was glad to hear from you and to know that you
were still alive, though your ears were frozen. I've got a piece of*

very wonderful news for you, that I am sure will be a great surprise. I am announcing my engagement to William Mitchell on July 16th.

To say I am the happiest girl on earth would be expressing it mildly and I wish you knew Bill so that you could know how very lucky I am.

The family are all East, but they have been marvelous about the whole thing, and now I am hoping to be able to persuade them that I must be married soon and go to Key West where Bill is stationed as ensign in naval aviation. Pardon the brevity of this but I wanted you to know first!

As Always,
Ginevra.

Scott managed to gather his wits and send this reply:

Hq. Co. 45th Inf.
Camp Sheridan Ala
July 21st, 1918

Dear Ginev:
This is to congratulate you— I dont know Billy Mitchell but from all I've heard of him he must be one of the best ever—
Doesn't it make you sigh with relief to be settled and think of all the men you escaped marrying?

As Ever
Scott

Fitzgerald did know Bill Mitchell. He had questioned Ginevra about him in a January 1915 letter, one of the first he ever wrote to her, and he had met Mitchell during one of the visits he made to Lake Forest. Probably it was the visit in August 1916; beside that date in his ledger Fitzgerald wrote "Beautiful Billy Mitchell."

The envelope for Scott's letter to Ginevra, congratulating her on her engagement to Bill Mitchell. The letter itself is facsimiled as part of the frontispiece of this book.

William Hamilton Mitchell was an ideal match for Ginevra. He was the son of John J. Mitchell, president of the Illinois Trust & Savings Bank and a board member of numerous Chicago and New York corporations. Bill's grandfather William H. Mitchell, for whom he was named, was a self-made man, like both of Ginevra's grandfathers and like Scott's Grandfather McQuillan. William H.

Mitchell had tried his luck in the California Gold Rush of 1849, then had returned to Illinois in 1852 to work for the Alton Packet Co., a steamship line. In the railroad boom of the 1860s he had struck out on his own and built the Alton & St. Louis Railway, a small but profitable operation. In 1874, at the age of fifty-seven, he had come to Chicago and had transformed himself into a banker, rising to first vice president of Illinois Trust. His son John (Ginevra's prospective father-in-law) became president of that institution after being allowed to work his own way up from the position of messenger boy.

The Mitchells and the Kings were family friends. Charles King and John Mitchell were business associates, with offices in the same building downtown. They collaborated on moneymaking ventures and socialized together at Onwentsia. Ginevra had known Bill for most of her life. In her diary she mentions evenings on which the Mitchells came over to her parents' house for dinner; sometimes Bill would stay and spend the night. Later he seems to have developed a crush on her; on January 2, 1915, according to her diary, he sent her flowers, and from time to time she notes on the diary pages that he has written to her at Westover.

Ginevra's marriage to Bill Mitchell was a dynastic affair very much approved by both sets of parents. In fact Bill's younger brother, Clarence, would marry Ginevra's younger sister Marjorie a few years later. Bill was intelligent, blond, and good-looking; he had left Harvard to enlist in the naval aviation corps, one of the most glamorous and dangerous branches of the armed forces. He proved to be an unusually good flyer; in July 1917, as a newly fledged ensign, he was assigned as a flight instructor at the naval air station in Key West, Florida. He proposed to Ginevra while he was home on leave, and she accepted.

Bill Mitchell posing in naval aviator gear, including bearskin mittens.

They were married in Chicago on September 4, 1918, at four o'clock in the afternoon, in St. Chrysostom's Episcopal Church. Fitzgerald received an invitation, which he later pasted into a scrapbook, but he probably did not attend. He did secure a published report of the wedding from one of the Chicago newspapers and pasted that into his scrapbook as well. The write-up, reproduced below, is filled with wartime superlatives:

The Triumph of Youth

What a realization of the supreme power of youth is forced on us by these so-called "war weddings." The old and

Arnold Genthe

MISS GINEVRA KING

Daughter of Mr. and Mrs. Charles Garfield King, of Chicago and Lake Forest. She is a Westover girl and would have been a debutante last winter, but the war took her father abroad and she decided to devote all her time to war work. She is a Junior League player and drives in the motor corps. The Kings will spend two months at Rye Beach.

11

Ginevra on the cover of the July 1918 Town and Country.
Her engagement was announced the same month.

wise look on with awe at the valorous determination of the young to snatch happiness from the tremendous conflagration which is burning up our outworn failure of a civilization. The flames light up the radiant faces of our boys and girls as, two by two, they join hands and smilingly undertake to cope with the great catastrophe. . . .

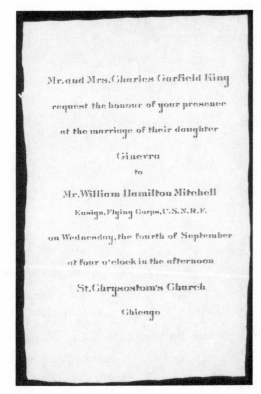

Mr. and Mrs. Charles Garfield King

request the honour of your presence

at the marriage of their daughter

Ginevra

to

Mr. William Hamilton Mitchell

Ensign, Flying Corps, U.S.N.R.F.

on Wednesday, the fourth of September

at four o'clock in the afternoon

St. Chrysostom's Church

Chicago

Scott's invitation to Ginevra's wedding, from his scrapbook.

But these are thoughts that only lurk in the outskirts of the mind. Last Wednesday at the marriage of Miss Ginevra King, daughter of Mr. and Mrs. Charles Garfield King, to Ensign William H. Mitchell, son of Mr. and Mrs. John J.

Mitchell, the extreme youth of the bridal couple, their gay and gallant air, their uncommon good looks, the distinguished appearance of both sets of parents, the smart frocks and becoming uniforms, all made an impression of something brilliant, charming, and cheerful. . . .

The carrying of the flag at the head of the wedding procession was a most impressive feature of the ceremony. As it was borne up the aisle every one stood up. Our flag means so inexpressibly much to us nowadays!

A gay reception at the Kings' utterly charming house, 1450 Astor street, followed. Every one said that there never was a more beautiful bride, or more stunning wedding presents. The former is a decided brunette and one of the prettiest, most attractive girls that ever came out of Chicago. The bridegroom, Ensign Mitchell, U.S.A., is as pronounced a blond as she is a brunette, and a good looking young aviator he makes.

Bill and Ginevra honeymooned in Florida, then took up residence briefly in Key West, near the air base. After the war ended in November, they returned to Lake Forest. Ginevra had managed to lose her engagement ring, but no one scolded her. To replace the ring, according to family lore, Bill's father purchased a large house for the young couple, a handsome Tudor-style limestone dwelling at 901 Rosemary Avenue in Lake Forest. Ginevra and Bill Mitchell would live in this house during their entire married life.

Fitzgerald, in Montgomery, now began a serious pursuit of Zelda. Perhaps Ginevra's wedding freed him to make an emotional segue to a new woman. In an act that was typical of him, he set an exact date for the transfer of emotion. In his ledger entry for

September 1918 he wrote, "Fell in love on the 7th." These dates are significant: he met Zelda in July 1918, the same month in which Ginevra wrote to announce her engagement; he fell in love with Zelda on September 7, 1918, three days after Ginevra became Mrs. William Mitchell. It's not surprising that, ever after, Fitzgerald mixed the two women in his fiction—and perhaps in his mind.

Early in November 1918, about a month after Ginevra's wedding, Fitzgerald was transferred to Camp Mills, Long Island, an embarkation point for troops headed to Europe. The war, however, ended on the eleventh, and Fitzgerald was sent back to Montgomery to await discharge. There he continued to court Zelda and eventually persuaded her to marry him, though they seem not to have had a formal engagement. After his discharge in February 1919, Fitzgerald went alone to New York, where he took a junior-level job in the advertising business and attempted, on the side, to write short stories for the commercial magazine market. He failed at both ventures. His work at the ad agency was stultifying, and he sold only two of his efforts ("Babes" and "The Debutante") to the magazines. The heroines of both pieces were based on Ginevra.

Zelda, waiting in Montgomery, lost faith in him and broke off their plans for marriage. Fitzgerald quit his advertising job in June, went on a month-long bender, and limped home to St. Paul in July 1919. There he set up a work table on the top floor of his parents' home and, in a six-week burst of hard labor, transformed *The Romantic Egotist* into *This Side of Paradise*. He assembled the manuscript in a rush of improvisation and fresh invention, had it typed up, and mailed it off to Scribners. The novel was accepted for publication on September 16th. Emboldened by this success, he returned to Montgomery and persuaded Zelda to renew their engagement. They were married in New York in a chapel of St.

Patrick's Cathedral on April 3, 1920, a week after Scribners published *This Side of Paradise*.

Scott sent a copy of the novel to Ginevra a few days before he married Zelda. In an accompanying letter he told Ginevra that he

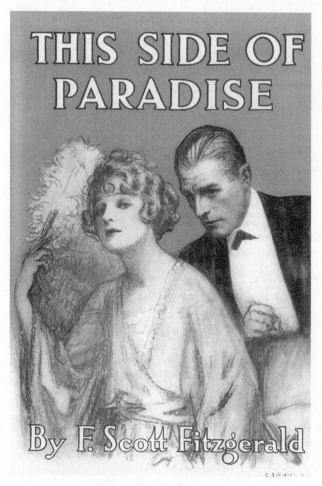

The jacket for This Side of Paradise, *Scott's first novel.*
Two characters in the book are based on Ginevra.

was about to be wed, but to judge from her reply on April 17th he was dodgy about Zelda's name and about other details:

Dear Scott:—

Your very nice present was a-waiting me on my return from California last Saturday, and I haven't written to thank you as I wished to read some of your book before I sent my congratulations to you.

I am enclosing a criticism from the Chicago Tribune, with whom you certainly seem to have an unholy drag—! I can hardly blame them though, for the book is a great success, I personally think. Also everyone seems to be speaking of it, and you have made a name for yourself. Not that I didn't think for a moment but that you eventually would, after receiving the Part I and Part II's for so long a time, but I cannot begin to tell you how really pleased I am at your success, so try to read between these incoherent lines and gather that I'm proud to know you!!

When next you are in Chicago, please come and see us. Telephone conversations are very unsatisfactory, especially as the last one we had was rudely interrupted by the yelling of my young son! He's quite a boy. You had better come up to see him, anyway, also to meet Bill—— By the way, who are you going to marry so shortly? Why didn't you tell me her name n'everything instead of mere insinuations? You're a funny one—

Many, many thanks to you, Scott, for remembering me, and I do wish you all the success in the world!

Always sincerely
Ginevra K. Mitchell

The review that Ginevra sent to Scott, clipped from the April 3rd *Chicago Daily Tribune,* was a rave by the book critic Burton Rascoe entitled "A Youth in the Saddle." *This Side of Paradise,* Rascoe wrote, gave Fitzgerald "a fair claim to membership in that small squad of contemporary American fictionists who are producing literature. It is sincere, it is honest, it is intelligent, it is handled in an individual manner, it bears the impress, it seems to me, of genius." Rascoe's review was by no means the only favorable notice that Fitzgerald received. *This Side of Paradise* enjoyed an excellent press, with mostly laudatory reviews and a few negative ones to stir controversy. Almost overnight Fitzgerald became a literary celebrity; he and Zelda would remain famous throughout the 1920s.

CHAPTER FIVE

Marriage

⬥✕⬥

Ginevra and Bill Mitchell settled into married life in Lake Forest. They prospered during the 1920s: he followed his father-in-law's example and became a stockbroker, co-founding the firm of Mitchell, Hutchins & Co. and enjoying much success in the postwar boom. Ginevra became a young society matron. At various times during the decade, the *Chicago Tribune* sent its photographers to take pictures of her—inspecting a model of a home for the indigent, tending fruit trees in her garden, wearing an elaborate headdress and gown for a society ball. She helped to organize and raise money for public charities, and she chaired the Illinois division of the Women's Organization for National Prohibition Reform—a group that wanted to repeal Prohibition. Ginevra developed into a good golfer, with an excellent short game, and she took up riding seriously, joining the Onwentsia Hunt and showing her mounts in competitions around Chicago. She rode sidesaddle, which requires a good deal of skill and athleticism. Photographs from the 1920s show her taking sixteen-hand thoroughbreds over four-foot fences—not an activity for the faint of heart.

Ginevra's life was not altogether charmed. On June 23, 1921, she gave birth to a second son; he was named Charles King Mitchell, for her father. The child had Down syndrome. "Buddy," as he was called, was born during the eugenics era, a period when he would have been called a "mongoloid idiot" by most people, including the doctors Ginevra and Bill consulted. The cause of Down syndrome

Ginevra in 1922, dressed for a formal dance.

(an extra chromosome) was not then known and would not be discovered until 1959. A child with Down syndrome prompted speculation about the mother and father: the condition was variously attributed to tuberculosis, thyroid imbalance, uterine exhaustion, neuropathic heredity, alcoholism, or syphilis in the parents.

Ginevra riding to hounds during the 1930s.

Buddy Mitchell was fortunate to be born into a family that could afford excellent care for him. He stayed at home, living with a caretaker on the top floor of the house on Rosemary Avenue. His sister, who was born five years after him, remembers him as a sweet, docile boy who came downstairs several times a day to see his parents and siblings. Buddy's presence did cause some problems. Ginevra and Bill Mitchell probably felt themselves to be under the scrutiny of their own parents, all four of whom lived nearby, and of their friends in Lake Forest, most of whom they had grown up with. Buddy represented, at least to outside observers, a flaw in the public face of their marriage. Ginevra's father accepted Buddy's condition and sympathized with Bill and Ginevra; Bill's father reacted in a different way, refusing ever to acknowledge that there was anything out of the ordinary about the boy and not allowing anyone within his hearing to suggest that there was.

Bill Mitchell's parents died in a car crash on October 29, 1927. His eventual inheritance from the estate made him and Ginevra financially secure. Bill had good instincts as a broker and built his and Ginevra's assets by investing them in the Chicago and New York stock markets during the months that followed. In February 1929, however, he sensed trouble and withdrew all of their money from both stock exchanges. Thus they were largely untouched by the crash in October. They preserved their wealth and rode out the 1930s without great difficulty. They were aware that many working-class people in Lake Forest had not been so fortunate. They operated what amounted to a soup kitchen from their home on Rosemary Avenue in the evenings, serving meals to the unemployed, many of whom had lately been servants in the houses of their friends.

Ginevra and Bill Mitchell stayed out of the newspapers. People of their social station were not eager for public notice during the Depression. Wealthy families in Chicago during the 1930s were vulnerable to the criminals who were then terrorizing the city. Kidnappings were frequent enough for rich men to hire bodyguards, and robberies were a constant threat.

On the evening of Saturday, November 21, 1931, Bill and Ginevra Mitchell were giving a dinner party for a group of their friends, including Peg Carry, one of the Big Four, who was now Mrs. Edward A. Cudahy, Jr. Also in attendance were Mr. and Mrs. Leslie Wheeler, Mr. and Mrs. William McCormick Blair, and several other couples. Dinner was over, and everyone was playing backgammon. At about 10:30 P.M., four armed thieves entered the Rosemary Avenue grounds and approached the main residence. They overpowered the night watchman and forced him to accompany them. Next they broke into a cottage occupied by the chauffeur, whose name was William Matheson, and compelled him and his wife to come along as well. A few minutes later, the robbers burst into the Mitchells' home. They rounded up everyone, including the house servants, and ordered the guests to put their money and jewelry on the dining-room table and to kneel on the floor. Ginevra was singled out as the woman of the house and was taken upstairs by two of the robbers. They went to her bedroom and made her give them her jewelry box, which they emptied.

Meanwhile, downstairs, the chauffeur had managed to slip out of the dining room unnoticed. He made his way to the second floor by a back staircase and found a telephone. He called the Lake Forest police and then hid under a bed. The police dispatcher sent two patrolmen to the house; one knocked on the front door while the other stayed outside, hidden in the yard. The thieves opened the door and took the first policeman prisoner but, in the excitement of the moment, forgot to disarm him.

The appearance of this policeman caused the robbers to lose their nerve. They took the valuables they had collected and fled from the house. The policeman inside pursued them, firing his revolver, and the policeman outside also began to shoot. The bandits returned fire, then scattered. In their flight they abandoned their getaway car and nearly all of the booty, which was later found inside the pockets of an overcoat that had snagged on a wire fence. Three of the gunmen were caught that night; the fourth fled Chicago but came back three years later and was arrested and imprisoned.

The story was on the front pages of the Chicago newspapers for the next two days, with loud headlines and numerous photos. "HOLD UP MANSION OF W.H. MITCHELL," read one scare head. "SEIZE 3; FIND $150,000 LOOT," read another. Ginevra and Bill were photographed leaving home to go downtown where they were to identify the recovered jewelry. In the photo Ginevra is wearing high heels and a chic hat and is smiling directly at the camera. All but two pieces of her jewelry were recovered. She was quoted in the reporter's account: "They forced me to accompany them to my room, where they took my jewelry and also demanded to be admitted to my children's rooms. I argued them out of that."*

These criminals, though inept, were dangerous. Ginevra and the others were fortunate. The chauffeur became a local hero, along with the two policemen who had answered the call for help. For Bill and Ginevra Mitchell, this was unaccustomed notoriety; they were not used to being in the spotlight.

Scott and Zelda Fitzgerald, by contrast, were comfortable in the public eye. He was famous as a writer and she as a personality. His short stories appeared regularly in the *Saturday Evening Post* and in other mass-circulation magazines. He published autobiographical pieces as well; in these he created public personalities for himself,

---

* "Mother was always cool in a tight spot." (Ginevra Hunter in conversation, December 26, 2003.)

Zelda, and their daughter, Scottie, who had been born in 1922. Zelda began to write for publication too—stories about young women of her generation and articles about current trends in behavior. Some of this writing appeared under her own byline; other pieces, which she composed and Scott revised, were published under both of their names. Scott wrote two more novels during the decade—*The Beautiful and Damned* in 1922 and *The Great Gatsby* in 1925—and published two substantial collections of short fiction. None of these books became bestsellers, but his short-story price with the *Post* continued to climb, reaching $4,000 per story by 1929, and his total earnings were substantial. Subsidiary rights from stage and movie adaptations brought in even more money.

The Fitzgeralds spent it all. They were at the center of the gaudy spree of the 1920s, living either in New York or on Long Island or, after 1924, as expatriates in Paris and on the French Riviera. They never owned a house or settled in one location. Instead they moved from place to place and lived in rented lodgings or luxury hotels. Fitzgerald was in and out of debt but was always able to rescue himself by producing short stories for the "slicks," as the mass-circulation magazines were called. Some of these narratives were mediocre formula fiction, but others were excellent work, with high stylistic polish and penetrating insight into human behavior.

In several of these stories, Fitzgerald used Ginevra as a model for the female lead. He was able to capture her beauty and charm on the printed page, and he could bring to life the bright shimmer of her social world—as he had seen it at eighteen and nineteen years of age. He probably kept up with the major events of her life through mutual friends, but he carefully avoided seeing her so that his illusions would remain undisturbed. Probably he knew that her second child had been abnormal. He was in Hollywood when the robbery at her house occurred; whether he read or heard about it is not known.

The Fitzgeralds lived a fast-paced, glamorous life until the late 1920s. By 1928 Zelda had become dissatisfied with her role in the marriage and had begun to study ballet seriously, training with a rigor and zeal that put great strain on her. Fitzgerald responded with erratic behavior and heavy drinking, though somehow he managed still to write well (and sometimes brilliantly) while failing in other areas of his life. As with the Mitchells, the Crash of 1929 did not touch Scott and Zelda. They had nothing invested in the stock market; indeed, they had no savings at all. His short-story prices with the *Post* and other magazines remained high, though, and outwardly he and Zelda seemed to be living glamorous lives. The collapse of their marriage began in April 1930, with the first of Zelda's mental breakdowns. From that time on, she was never entirely well or whole again, and for the rest of her life she was in and out of mental institutions. Fitzgerald persevered with his writing, but his health deteriorated and his drinking increased.

During a period of stability in 1933, Zelda left the Phipps Clinic at Johns Hopkins, where she was being treated as an outpatient, and traveled to Chicago with a hired companion to see the World's Fair there. Fitzgerald decided that she should meet Ginevra. He was still optimistic that Zelda would recover entirely and probably thought that she and Ginevra would enjoy getting to know each other. He telephoned Ginevra long-distance and asked her to entertain Zelda. Ginevra agreed to take her to lunch. The occasion, Ginevra later remembered, did not go well; Zelda was at first loquacious but soon lapsed into silence, and for the remainder of the luncheon Ginevra had to carry the conversation alone. Surely Zelda knew that Ginevra had been Scott's first love, and probably she had some idea of how important Ginevra had been to him in his creative life. Zelda must also have been acutely conscious of how different her own current state was from Ginevra's. Fitzgerald's idea of bringing them together was probably not a good one.

Fitzgerald was struggling to finish a novel of expatriate life that he had begun in 1925. Finally he did so, publishing it in April 1934 as *Tender Is the Night*. The book was a critical and commercial disappointment. Reviews were mixed, and the novel sold only about 13,000 copies, barely enough to earn back his advances from Scribners. In 1935 and 1936, he endured a harrowing "Crack-Up" period in North Carolina; the following year he went to Hollywood as a scriptwriter for Metro-Goldwyn-Mayer in an effort to recoup his finances and salvage his career.

Ginevra probably knew some of these details. She would surely have been aware of Scott's fame as a writer, and she must have seen reviews, photographs, and interviews with him in newspapers and magazines. Perhaps she kept up with the progress of his life through friends in St. Paul. How much of his work she read is not known. She was not a literary person; people who knew her do not remember her as a regular reader of fiction, nor do they recall her ever discussing Fitzgerald's work. Probably she was unaware of how important, to Fitzgerald, his memories of her had become.

❧

SCOTT AND Ginevra saw each other one last time, in October 1937. He was writing movie scripts for MGM in Hollywood, and she was in California to see Buddy, who had been placed in a special school in Santa Barbara. Through a mutual friend, Josephine Ordway of St. Paul, Scott had learned that Ginevra was planning to visit. He contacted her and suggested that they get together. She agreed—but admitted later that she was nervous about the reunion. Scott was apprehensive too and confessed his fears to his daughter, Scottie, in a letter dated October 8th:

> She was the first girl I ever loved and I have faithfully avoided seeing her up to this moment to keep that illusion perfect, because she ended up by throwing me over with the most supreme boredom and indifference. I don't know whether I should go or not. It would be very, very strange. These great beauties are often something else at thirty-eight, but Ginevra had a great deal besides beauty.

By now Ginevra's marriage was nearing its end. She and Bill Mitchell had been a good match initially and had been kept together by the ties between their families and by their children. By 1937, however, their marriage was essentially over. Perhaps Fitzgerald knew this, perhaps not. Ginevra might or might not have known about the status of his marriage—which had itself become largely epistolary. He and Zelda exchanged long, heartfelt letters but rarely saw each other.

Initially Ginevra asked Scott to come to Santa Barbara for a dinner party at a friend's house on Saturday, October 9th. He begged off, so she traveled to Hollywood to see him on the eleventh. They met for lunch at the Beverly Wilshire Hotel, where she was staying. At first the occasion went well, with much reminiscing. Fitzgerald had no alcohol at lunch; he told her that he had been on the wagon for several months. After the check had been paid, however, he went into the hotel bar with her to wait for one of her friends, who was to meet her there. He began ordering drinks—double shots of gin with Tom Collins, she later remembered. At this point they began discussing his fiction, and she asked him which characters he had based on her. "Which bitch do you think you are?" he said. On this note the reunion ended.

Ginevra returned to Santa Barbara the next day. Scott resumed work on a screenplay called *Three Comrades,* based on the novel of that title by the German writer Erich Maria Remarque, author of *All Quiet on the Western Front.* Scott telephoned Ginevra several times in Santa Barbara, but nothing came of the calls. He had met the Hollywood newspaper columnist Sheilah Graham several months earlier and had begun the close relationship with her that would last until his death, in December 1940.

Fitzgerald wrote one last story about himself and Ginevra. He based it on their reunion in Hollywood—and, fairly obviously, on her March 1916 story, which he must have reread once more. He called his story "Three Hours between Planes" and sold it to *Esquire,* where it appeared in July 1941, seven months after his death.*

The protagonist of "Three Hours between Planes," whose name is Donald Plant, unexpectedly finds himself in the hometown of a former flame. He is in the small airport there, waiting for his next flight, and has some time on his hands. On an impulse he telephones the woman, whose name is Nancy Gifford, and finds her at home. She invites him to come over: "I was just sitting here," she says, "having a highball by myself." Donald takes a taxi to her house and finds her waiting, "a dark-haired little beauty standing against the lighted door, a glass in her hand." She is married, but her husband is away.

Nancy and Donald sit and talk: he reminds her of times in the past when they were together, but she cannot seem to remember

---

* "Three Hours between Planes" is reprinted in *The Stories of F. Scott Fitzgerald,* ed. Malcolm Cowley (New York: Scribners, 1951): 477–82.

them. Still, he is charming and she is lonely. They kiss. At this point the narrative takes a turn that Fitzgerald seems to have borrowed from the moment in Ginevra's 1916 story when "Scott Fitz-Gerald" consults his file of notes on former girlfriends. Nancy opens an old album and shows Donald a photograph of himself as a child. He realizes that the photo is of someone else, a boy named Donald Bowers. Nancy has confused their names and has been under the impression that she has been kissing Donald Bowers. She does not even remember Donald Plant. He tries to kiss her again, but she refuses and he departs. He catches his flight at the airport, and as the plane rises into the night he reflects on what he has lost—his memory of Nancy as a girl and his fantasy that they might someday meet and fall in love as adults. His impulse to call her had been a mistake.

Ginevra's marriage lasted only a little longer; she and Bill Mitchell were divorced in 1939, the same year that their son Buddy died. He had been taken to the Golden Gate International Exposition in San Francisco, where he caught a cold that developed into pneumonia. After the divorce Ginevra withdrew for a time from Chicago society, then married John T. Pirie, Jr., who would become the chairman of Carson, Pirie, Scott & Co., the well-known Chicago department store. This marriage was successful: friends remember Ginevra and John Pirie as well-matched and happy together.

Ginevra died in 1980 at the age of eighty-two, having outlived Fitzgerald by almost exactly forty years. She rarely spoke about him. She had no desire to participate in his posthumous fame—which, by the 1970s, had become enormous. Several new biographies and memoirs were published during that decade, as was Nancy Milford's life of Zelda. Numerous academic studies ap-

peared; a much-publicized movie version of *The Great Gatsby,* star-
ring Mia Farrow and Robert Redford, was released in 1974.
Ginevra, however, did not attempt to trade on her connection with
Fitzgerald. She was content to let her letters and diary stay in her
closet.

CHAPTER SIX

The "Ginevra" Characters

Fitzgerald copied nothing from Ginevra's letters, but he did use them to recapture memories of her and her world. Reading the letters seems to have stimulated his emotions and imagination, reminding him of his intense, youthful love for her and of his social insecurities when he visited Lake Forest. The letters surely called into memory the resentments he had felt over slights and snubs, real or imagined. He knew instinctively that much of his best writing came from early feelings of inferiority and failure: Ginevra's letters would have provided him with passage back into those years and those emotions.

Fitzgerald based a great many characters on Ginevra. In 1935 an anthologist named Vernon McKenzie asked him to comment on Judy Jones, the female protagonist of "Winter Dreams." Fitzgerald wrote that Judy had been based on "my first girl 18–20 whom I've used over and over and never forgotten." The phrase "over and over" is accurate. Beginning with "Babes in the Woods," written in 1917, and ending with "Three Hours between Planes," composed in 1939, Fitzgerald drew repeatedly on his memories of Ginevra.

Between 1920, when he began as a professional, and 1940, when he died, Fitzgerald published four novels and more than 160 short stories, an impressive record. Ginevra is the basis for characters in two of the novels, *This Side of Paradise* (1920) and *The Great Gatsby* (1925), but it is in the stories that her presence is most strongly felt. Short fiction published in high-paying, mass-circulation magazines

Fitzgerald in profile, about 1925.

was Fitzgerald's most dependable source of income. His stories were written in quick bursts of literary energy, paid for in advance of publication, and published soon after they had been composed. Though Fitzgerald wrote these stories for money, he also used them to experiment with characters, settings, themes, and plots that would later appear in his novels.

He turned to Ginevra repeatedly in his short fiction, and most often in those stories that he chose *not* to include in the four cloth-bound collections that he published during his career—*Flappers and Philosophers* (1920), *Tales of the Jazz Age* (1922), *All the Sad Young Men* (1926), and *Taps at Reveille* (1935). In many of these uncollected (and therefore lesser-known) stories, Fitzgerald wrote about a failed romance between a poor boy and a rich girl, often followed by a reunion between the two characters years later. In the early stories, the ones he published during the 1920s, the man is usually taken away by the war. Sometimes he returns as a damaged battlefield hero and is reunited with a heroine whose social status has fallen. In other narratives the hero leaves to make his fortune through business derring-do, then returns as a wealthy man and is reunited with the rich girl. Sometimes a new love springs up, more mature and realistic than the first infatuation; more often the reunion generates no sparks, suggesting that first love cannot be recaptured and repeated. These patterns are found also in stories that Fitzgerald wrote during the 1930s, though now the plot device that separates the young lovers is the Depression, not the war. Otherwise the mechanics of the stories are the same.

Fitzgerald worked repeated variations on these plots and themes, but he reprinted only two of the stories. "The Jelly-Bean" (1920) appeared in *Tales of the Jazz Age,* and "Winter Dreams" (1922) in *All the Sad Young Men.* The other stories were never collected: "Dice, Brassknuckles and Guitar" (1923), "Diamond Dick" (1924), "The Third Casket" (1924), "The Unspeakable Egg" (1924), "John Jackson's Arcady" (1924), "Love in the Night" (1925), "Not in the Guidebook" (1925), "A Penny Spent" (1926), "Presumption" (1926), "The

Adolescent Marriage" (1926), "The Love Boat" (1927), "Flight and Pursuit" (1932), "The Rubber Check" (1932), "More than Just a House" (1933), and "New Types" (1934).*

Fitzgerald chose not to reprint these stories because he wanted variation within each collection, but he must also not have wanted to reveal how much he relied on these characters and plot devices. He did admit to his dependence in a 1933 essay on literary inspiration called "One Hundred False Starts":

> Mostly, we authors must repeat ourselves—that's the truth. We have two or three great and moving experiences in our lives—experiences so great and moving that it doesn't seem at the time that anyone else has been so caught up and pounded and dazzled and astonished and beaten and broken and rescued and illuminated and rewarded and humbled in just that way ever before. . . . Then we learn our trade, well or less well, and we tell our two or three stories—each time in a new disguise—maybe ten times, maybe a hundred, as long as people will listen.

Ginevra is also the model for an important character in three of the Basil Duke Lee stories and for the lead character in all five of the Josephine Perry stories—two series that Fitzgerald published in the *Saturday Evening Post* in the late 1920s and early 1930s. With an irony that he must surely have appreciated, Fitzgerald's youthful

---

* These stories were variously reprinted after Fitzgerald's death in three collections: Cowley's edition of *The Stories of F. Scott Fitzgerald*; *Bits of Paradise*, ed. Matthew J. Bruccoli and Scottie Fitzgerald Smith (New York: Scribners, 1974); and *The Price Was High*, ed. Matthew J. Bruccoli (New York: Harcourt Brace Jovanovich, 1979).

romance with Ginevra, a child of wealth, became an essential part of his professional capital. He drew on his memories of her repeatedly during his career, writing stories that earned him many thousands of dollars. The lowest price he received for any one of these stories was $1,500 for "Diamond Dick"; the highest was $4,000 for "Flight and Pursuit" and for several of the Basil stories. If nothing else, his romance with Ginevra had been a good investment.

Like most writers, Fitzgerald created composite characters. Only a few of his most memorable characters were based on single models. In *This Side of Paradise*, Thayer Darcy is based entirely on Sigourney Fay, and Thomas Parke D'Invilliers is a portrait of the poet John Peale Bishop. In *The Beautiful and Damned*, Gloria is a version of Zelda; in "Babylon Revisited," a 1932 short story, Marian Peters is closely modeled after Rosalind Smith, Zelda's sister. Kathleen Moore in *The Last Tycoon* is drawn entirely from Sheilah Graham. But most of Fitzgerald's other characters, if not wholly invented, are composites. He created Jay Gatsby as a blend of Max von Gerlach, Joseph G. Robin, and himself. Dick Diver in *Tender Is the Night* is drawn from Gerald Murphy, Walker Ellis, Theodore Chanler, and himself. Nicole Diver is based in nearly equal parts on Sara Murphy and on Zelda. Monroe Stahr in *The Last Tycoon* is a fictional portrait of Irving Thalberg and, less obviously, Maxwell Perkins.

For the "Ginevra" characters, Fitzgerald seems always to have begun with a visual image of her and then to have mixed in additional traits of personality. Isabelle Borgé in "Babes in the Woods" and *This Side of Paradise*, for example, is modeled on Ginevra, but her conscious scheming and her theatricality are more features of Fitzgerald's own personality than of Ginevra's. Rosalind Connage in *This Side of Paradise* is a blending of Ginevra and Zelda. Rosalind's matter-of-fact attitude about marriage is taken from Ginevra, but her rebelliousness and unconventionality are patterned after Zelda. Kismine Washington in "The Diamond as Big as the Ritz" is a fantasy figure; her cold-blooded attitude toward the playmates who are brought in to amuse her and are then "put to sleep" is surely Fitzgerald's interpretation of similar behavior he thought he saw in Ginevra—but he must have seen it in other rich friends who invited him home for holidays while he was at the Newman School and at Princeton. Judy Jones, the femme fatale in "Winter Dreams," is drawn from Fitzgerald's imagined picture of Ginevra as a young girl, but Judy also resembles Zelda.

Daisy Buchanan is a composite. Like Ginevra, Daisy has dark hair and a memorable voice; like Ginevra she is unhappy in her marriage. She has been a part of the Lake Forest world and is protected by money and social status. Daisy's aimlessness and insouciance, however, seem to come from elsewhere. Her wartime romance with Jay Gatsby is based on Fitzgerald's courtship of Zelda. Daisy's comment when her daughter is born—"I hope she'll be a fool . . . a beautiful little fool!"—is also taken from Zelda, though another of Zelda's comments, the one about irresponsible driving ("It takes two to make an accident . . ."), is given to Jordan Baker, who is based on Edith Cummings.

Fitzgerald's most sympathetic rendering of Ginevra is as the elaborately (and somewhat comically) named Ermine Gilberte Labouisse Bibble in the Basil Duke Lee stories, an excellent series that Fitzgerald published in the *Saturday Evening Post* in 1928 and 1929.* Basil is much enamored of "Minnie" Bibble, but she does not quite sense the

---

* *The Basil and Josephine Stories*, ed. Jackson R. Bryer and John Kuehl (New York: Scribners, 1973). The quotations that follow are from this edition and will be cited parenthetically.

depth of his emotion. Perhaps such feelings are beyond her. Fitzgerald does not condemn Minnie or judge her: he seems to realize that the problem is with Basil, who is a version of himself as a teenager. Basil is intensely romantic, and he has a bothersome tendency to invest others with feelings and reactions that they do not actually possess. Part of the satisfaction of reading the Basil stories is in seeing Basil come to these realizations about himself without losing his innate romanticism or his capacity for hope and love.

Minnie Bibble appears in three of the nine Basil stories: "He Thinks He's Wonderful," "Forging Ahead," and "Basil and Cleopatra." Minnie is a Southern girl from New Orleans, but little else about her suggests Zelda Sayre. Basil meets Minnie when she pays a visit to a school friend in his hometown of St. Paul. We are made aware of Minnie's beauty in the very first description of her: "She was of a radiant freshness; her head had reminded otherwise not illiterate young men of damp blue violets, pierced with blue windows that looked into a bright soul, with today's new roses showing through" (126). The narrator turns to Minnie's smile:

> She looked at Basil, a childish open look; then opened her eyes wider as if she had some sort of comic misgivings, and smiled. . . . For all the candor of this smile, its effect, because of the special contours of Minnie's face and independent of her mood, was of sparkling invitation. Whenever it appeared Basil seemed to be suddenly inflated and borne upward, a little farther each time, only to be set down when the smile had reached a point where it must become a grin, and chose instead to melt away. It was like a drug. In a little while he wanted nothing except to watch it with a vast buoyant delight. (126–27)

In "The Freshest Boy," Minnie and Basil begin a romance in St. Paul, but Basil makes a misstep by boasting of his accomplishments to Minnie and her father. He learns a lesson: not to talk too much about himself and to let his behavior speak instead. Minnie reappears a year later in "Forging Ahead" when she returns to St. Paul for another visit. She and Basil are reunited at a country-club dance, but Basil is stuck with Rhoda Sinclair, an unattractive girl whom he has agreed to escort for the evening. Midway through the dance he manages to slip away; he finds Minnie, and they wander onto a veranda overlooking a lake. Basil has a chance to kiss Minnie, and she is willing, but he cannot bring himself to act:

Judy Jones from "Winter Dreams," as rendered by Arthur William Brown, the illustrator for Metropolitan *magazine. Ginevra was the model for Judy.*

In a curious panic he jumped to his feet. He couldn't possibly kiss her like this—right at once. It was all so different and older than a year ago. He was too excited to do more than walk up and down and say, "Gosh, I certainly am glad to see you," supplementing this unoriginal statement with an artificial laugh. (192)

The moment passes, and the dance comes to an end. Later that week Basil sees Minnie again, and again they manage to be alone, this time on the front porch of a friend's house. Fitzgerald bases the dialogue in the scene on Ginevra's letter to him of January 20, 1915, the full text of which is included in Appendix Two of this book:

> Suddenly she was whispering in his arms. "You're first, Basil—nobody but you."
>
> "You just admitted you were a flirt."
>
> "I know, but that was years ago. I used to like to be called fast when I was thirteen or fourteen, because I didn't care what people said; but about a year ago I began to see there was something better in life—honestly, Basil—and I've tried to act properly. But I'm afraid I'll never be an angel." (196)

Basil ponders her words for a moment, then listens as she continues:

> "I really haven't got such a line as everybody thinks, Basil, for I mean a lot of what I say way down deep, and nobody believes me. You know how much alike we are, and in a boy it doesn't matter, but a girl has to control her feelings, and that's hard for me, because I'm emotional." (197)

Minnie's final appearance comes in "Basil and Cleopatra," the last story of the series. By this point Basil has idealized her past all imagining and is conscious only of her beauty and charm, not of her inconstancy:

> Wherever she was became a beautiful and enchanted place to Basil, but he did not think of it that way. He thought the fascination was inherent in the locality, and long afterward a commonplace street or the mere name of a city would exude a peculiar glow, a sustained sound, that struck his soul alert with delight. In her presence he was too absorbed to notice his surroundings; so that her absence never made them empty, but, rather, sent him seeking for her through haunted rooms and gardens that he had never really seen before. (202)

Basil views Minnie through a haze of romanticism; it does not occur to him that she might have eyes for other boys:

> This time, as usual, he saw only the expression of her face, the mouth that gave an attractive interpretation of any emotion she felt or pretended to feel—oh, invaluable mouth— and the rest of her, new as a peach and old as sixteen. He was almost unconscious that they stood in a railroad station and entirely unconscious that she had just glanced over his shoulder and fallen in love with another young man. Turning to walk with the rest to the car, she was already acting for the stranger; no less so because her voice was pitched for Basil and she clung to him, squeezing his arm. (202)

The stranger for whom Minnie is performing is Littleboy Le Moyne, the scion of an old Southern family and, by the next day, the object of Minnie's wandering affections. Basil has quickly become only another of her many admirers. "I loved your letters," she tells him. "You're the best friend I have, Basil" (204–05). He has come all the way to Mobile, Alabama, to see Minnie one last time before he reports to Yale for his freshman year. He expects special attention but finds that he is only another young man in the stag line.

That fall Basil travels from New Haven to visit Minnie at Miss Beecher's School, where she is enrolled. As Minnie comes to meet him he is conscious yet again of her beauty: "Radiant and glowing, more mysteriously desirable than ever, wearing her very sins like stars, she came down to him in her plain white uniform dress, and his heart turned over at the kindness of her eyes" (211). Their meeting must take place in a "glass parlor," as at Westover; he is aware of the artificiality of the situation and of her fading affections for him. Later, back at Yale, he receives a photograph from Minnie, but she has made a mistake and sent him the photo meant for Littleboy, with a romantic inscription on the back.

Revenge comes for Basil on the football field. In the last game of the season, he is quarterbacking the Yale freshmen in a contest against Princeton. Littleboy, as fictional necessity would have it, is on the Princeton team; he is a defensive end, tall and aggressive. In the fourth quarter, with the score tied, Basil tricks Littleboy into rushing him, then throws the winning touchdown pass to his receiver. Victory is sweet, but as Basil knows by now, there will be no romantic reward later with Minnie—as, in his dreams, there should be. He sees her at a dance that night but resists the temptation to pursue her. "He had made all his mistakes for this time," he thinks (222). Basil leaves the dance and walks out on a veranda to be alone. There follows one of the most evocative passages in all of Fitzgerald's fiction:

> There was a flurry of premature snow in the air and the stars looked cold. Staring up at them he saw that they were his stars as always—symbols of ambition, struggle and glory. The wind blew through them, trumpeting that high white note for which he always listened, and the thin-blown clouds, stripped for battle, passed in review. The scene was of an unparalleled brightness and magnificence, and only the practiced eye of the commander saw that one star was no longer there. (222)

Fitzgerald's least sympathetic portrayal of Ginevra is found in the five Josephine Perry stories, published in 1930–31 as another series for the *Post*. Fitzgerald wrote these narratives shortly after Zelda had suffered her first breakdown and while he was struggling to pay the bills for her psychiatric treatment. He wanted to finish *Tender Is the Night* and had lost interest in the young female characters who had populated his short stories for so long—creatures like Ardita Farnam in "The Offshore Pirate," Rags Martin-Jones in "Rags Martin-Jones and the Pr-nce of W-les," and Nancy Lamar in "The Jelly-Bean." Josephine Perry shows the effects of Fitzgerald's disillusionment. She is selfish and vain; she uses people for her own purposes and likes to engage in shallow romances. Her punishment is to squander her emotional capital on flirtations and to lose the capacity for love.

The Basil stories, though narrated by an omniscient voice, are always presented through Basil's eyes and from his point of view. This approach creates sympathy and affection for Minnie Bibble, who is seen through the filter of Basil's romantic feelings. The Josephine stories, by contrast, come to us entirely from the perspective of a third-person narrator. There is no romantic coloration: this narrator is impersonal, analytical, and judgmental, with little inclination to excuse Josephine for her transgressions. He attempts to understand her treatment of others but finds it difficult. "Great beauty has a need, almost an obligation, of trying itself," the narrator tells us, but the insight generates little sympathy or forgiveness (242).

Fitzgerald wrote five stories about Josephine Perry: "First Blood," "A Nice Quiet Place," "A Woman with a Past," "A Snobbish Story," and "Emotional Bankruptcy." In three of them he used events from his romance with Ginevra. "A Nice Quiet Place" is loosely based on Ginevra's rustication at Biddeford Pool during the summer of 1915; "A Snobbish Story" is a fictional version, much altered, of her "firing" from Westover; "Emotional Bankruptcy" is modeled on her only visit to Princeton, in November 1916. In several of the stories, Fitzgerald includes letters written by Josephine to her friends and suitors, but the letters are inventions. Nothing in them comes from Ginevra King's letters, not even a re-creation of her voice.

At various points in the stories, Fitzgerald's narrator presents statements about Josephine's behavior. The statements are moralistic, hortatory, and unconvincing. In "A Woman with a Past," Josephine is resentful about the disapproval of others: "A girl earned her popularity by being beautiful and charming. The more beautiful and charming she was, the more she could afford to disregard public opinion" (269). Later in the same story Josephine is lectured by the narrator: "There were two kinds of men," she is told, "those you played with and those you might marry. . . . One mustn't run through people, and, for the sake of a romantic half-hour, trade a possibility that might develop—quite seriously—

later, at the proper time" (283). In "A Snobbish Story," Josephine has become bored by most of the men who pursue her: "The strong ones were dull, the clever ones were shy, and all too soon they were responding to Josephine with a fatal sameness, a lack of temperament that blurred their personalities" (292). In this story Josephine toys with the affections of a fledgling playwright named John Bailey, an amusing but penniless would-be writer who encourages her aspirations for the stage. The flirtation is quashed by her parents, who find Bailey unsuitable. Josephine comes quickly to agree and in so doing throws in her lot "with the rich and powerful of this world forever" (308).

Josephine's decision renders her insensitive to the hurt she causes in others. Paul Dempster, a Princeton boy in "Emotional Bankruptcy," is an example. "He had been devoted to Josephine for a year—long after her own interest had waned—he had long lost any power of judging her objectively; she had become simply a projection of his own dreams, a radiant, nebulous mass of light" (311). Later in this story Josephine finally meets a man to whom she is strongly drawn, a war hero named Edward Dicer, who has won honor as a member of the French aviation forces. Josephine responds powerfully to him but finds that she cannot summon even a counterfeit of love. She has used up her emotional resources. "Oh, what have I done to myself?" she wonders. The narrator now states the concluding moral of the series: "One cannot both spend and have. The love of her life had come by, and looking in her empty basket, she had found not a flower left for him—not one" (327).

GINEVRA KING eventually became an abstraction for Fitzgerald. He did not watch her grow older; in his mind the sadnesses and blows of life did not touch her. Zelda, on the other hand, was always before him. He observed her as she lost her youthful bloom, then watched her drift through the 1920s with little direction or purpose. One of the most unpleasant aspects of *The Beautiful and Damned* is the deterioration of Gloria's personality, which Fitzgerald patterned after changes that he saw in Zelda. Later, in the 1930s, Fitzgerald watched Zelda lose her mental equilibrium and documented that decline in *Tender Is the Night*. Ginevra, however, remained impervious to change, preserved within his memories.

Ginevra King represented one of several failures that occurred in Fitzgerald's life in 1917–19. He failed academically and socially at Princeton; he accomplished little of consequence during the war; he failed to have *The Romantic Egotist* accepted by Scribners; he was a bust in the advertising game; he sold only a few of his literary efforts on the magazine market; and he was unable to win Zelda's loyalty and commitment. Most people during these years thought of him as a lightweight, amusing to be around but with no serious chance for success. Ginevra presumably came to feel that way about him too. He had not measured up for her as a suitor; she liked to trade letters with him and to have him as a friend, but that was all.

And then, in September 1919, Fitzgerald's star began to shine. Scribners took *This Side of Paradise* for publication; Zelda agreed to renew their engagement; the magazine editors began to buy his stories; his novel was published to excellent reviews and strong sales; he became an overnight literary celebrity. These victories, however, never erased the bitterness of the early defeats. Fitzgerald wanted to remember those defeats; he understood that some of his best writing was about loss and regret, and he needed a way, a device, to bring back those emotions. Ginevra's letters, and his memories of her, were one method of recapturing the uncertain, romantic, desirous, ambitious young man he once had been.

In an odd but important way, what we now know about Fitzgerald's romance with Ginevra takes pressure off Zelda as the model for his heroines. Zelda Sayre was the most important woman in his life—his greatest love, his wife, his muse, his obsession. But from an artistic standpoint, Ginevra King was nearly as important to him as Zelda. Ginevra gave him access, early on, to a world of money and privilege that he might not otherwise have observed.

The Sayres were not wealthy people: Zelda's father was a judge, though not a particularly prominent one, and her family lived modestly in a rented dwelling, just as Fitzgerald's family did. Nor were the Sayres from an old, aristocratic Southern clan. Their social status and income did not begin to approach that of the Kings. It was through his romance with Ginevra, not Zelda, that Fitzgerald came into contact for the first time with the very rich and learned some of his earliest and most valuable lessons about them. When the rich were young they liked to divert themselves with friends from less elevated social ranks—perhaps during school holidays or summer vacations—but they knew not to allow flirtations or friendships to develop beyond a certain point. The role of the outsider (his own role during his visits to Chicago and Lake Forest) was to be amusing to his hosts, to pay attention to the less attractive girls, and to be impressed by the surroundings. Marriage into this world was only a distant possibility. If a prospective partner could bring something fresh into the family—new money, an old and respectable name, an inherited English title—then perhaps a marriage might be arranged. But good looks, an amusing line, and literary talent were not enough. For the very rich, these conventions of behavior carried through into adult life. They brought outsiders into their world for amusement and dalliance but were careful not to grant them full admission.

✻

WHENEVER FITZGERALD called Ginevra King into his memory, she stimulated emotions that were valuable to him as a writer. He surely remembered his youthful love for her, but he must have recalled even more keenly the frustrations that he had felt when he had visited her in Lake Forest. His memories of Ginevra's beauty remained fresh, and he imparted much of her allure to his heroines, but these characters cannot be touched. They remain remote and safe behind barriers of wealth, privilege, and high social standing.

What did Ginevra remember of Scott? Perhaps he truly was only one among many former admirers. But the intensity of her letters to him in 1915 and the feelings that she recorded in her diary suggest otherwise, as does the story that she wrote for him in 1916. During the earliest, best months of their romance, his letters touched her heart, and her love for him was fresh and new. As an adult she did not attempt to capitalize on her romance with Scott Fitzgerald, but it must have pleased her, at least a little, to know that he had become a major writer, that she had been his first love, and that he had never forgotten her.

A P P E N D I X E S

SELECTED DIARY ENTRIES

The entries from Ginevra's diary in this appendix begin in June 1914, about six months before she met Scott.

June 25

1914—Thursday. Stayed in bed all morning and arranged about a dance I'm giving on July 10th. There are to be 83 or 84 people. Courtney came over, and we wrote all the bids. After lunch we went down in her car and posted them all. Then she took me back to the house. Went to the Club to play golf with Rus. Edith + Peg came over later in the aft. Had supper + went to bed.

June 27

1914—Saturday. Went to Peg's with her about nine o'clock in the machine. We went all over town in her machine + had a general good time. I had lunch at her house, + right afterward John, Rus, Deering, Ralph + Stew came over to watch Rus + Peg practice the

Maxixe + Deering + I the one-step for the vaudeville show we're
going to give. At 4 o'clock was the first rehearsal, + I am to play
the guitar, dance with either Mark or Deering, + also be in a
chorus. Peg + I went to the Club + were joined there by numerous
others. Then we four went to French's + got a soda. Peg took me
home. Had supper at home, + went to bed early.

July 10

1914 Friday— Courtney came over at 9.30 in the morn. House in a
beastly turmoil on account of the dance. The Mitchells arrived at
10 o'clock. Thrills. 52–0. Billy brought me a huge bunch of
orchids from their hothouse! Went for a long ride in Jack's Loco*
before lunch. . . . Went to Fort Sheridan to watch a drill of the
Illinois National Guard but we were too late. Went + played tennis
at the Club. Got a soda, took C. home, went home, fooled around.
The Cudahy's for dinner + my dance afterwards. The house +
grounds looked wonderful. Lanterns everywhere. Great fun. Billy
+ the Mitchells spent the night.

July 18

1914 Saturday— Slept late + went to a rehearsal at 10 o'clock.
Everything is getting on fairly well now. Courtney came for lunch.
Had a shampoo. Peg came over + Mother started our costume,
mine is to be green chiffon + Peg's "a la Mrs Castle."† Then we

---

* The Locomobile, a luxury car of the period.

† The dancer Irene Castle who, with her husband, Vernon, originated the "Castle
  Walk," a popular prewar dance step.

went to the Club. Watched the Australian-Canadian tennis players practice for a while, had tea on the porch and then danced there in the club-house. Came home, had supper + "au lit."

July 26

Sunday 1914— Went in swimming over at Mrs. Thorne's in the morn. + stayed to lunch. There were about 30 people there, including Fowler, Bud + Louis Seaverns, Alex. McKinloch. . . . After lunch A. McK. + Bud took me over to Courtney and then the B.F. went down to Highland Park + had our pictures taken together. We came back + were initiated into the Big Four Club. Went home with Peg. Had supper + went to bed early—

July 29

Wednesday 1914. Went to the Club in the morning with Edith. Played golf with Deering, Fowler + Peg. Home with Edith for lunch. Tennis tournament in the afternoon. Edith + I played in the women's doubles to-gether + got beaten 6–1, 6–1. Went home with the Winters, who spent the night. Had a small supper party of Peg, Edith, Court, Deering, John, Edwin, Dan + Uncle Harry. Big Four rings came, also pictures. Then McLaughlin's masquerade. Went in Mother's Russian costume. Wonderful time. D. gave Martha Granger the heavy rush.

July 30

1914 Thursday. In the morning Dan, Edwin + I went to the Club, and after sitting around a while played tennis with B. Hubbard.

Edith watched us for a while, then played golf with Fowler. Had something to drink on the porch + then went home for lunch. Had a shampoo. Went to the Club to watch the tennis and Edith + I played. I beat her 6–1, 6–1, 6–4. Then we watched Billy F., John, Selby + Peg play for fun. Said goodbye to Fowler, Courtney + Harry Knott. Home for supper + bed. Poor Father is so worried about his business as the war seems pretty certain. Oh, how I hope it turns out all right!

August 8

1914 Saturday. Stayed at home till 12.00 o'clock in the morning, then went over to Mrs. Thorne's in swimming. . . . Had great fun. Lunch at Thorne's afterwards. Took Billy + Deering to the Club. Met Peg + Edith + we went for a ride, came back to the Club, hung around + later danced. Fowler came back again! Home for supper— After supper, Mother, Father, Mr. Cudahy + I went over to the Club + watched the dancing for a long while, then just as we were leaving, Mother let me dance one piece around the floor with Deering. It was too wonderful. "A Perfect Day." Went home + to bed.

September 22

Tuesday—1914— [Ginevra is stopping over in New York City on her way back to Westover.] Shopped almost all morning. Had lunch at the Ritz with Uncle Herman + Aunt Alice + Celia Jade. Then went straight to the 2 o'clock train. Saw everyone again. Great!! Got to school about 5 o'clock. Took an auto out. Bed early.

September 23

Wednesday. Miss Hillard talked all morning, partly to the new girls + to everybody. I am to take singing. Unpacked all afternoon and at five had my first singing lesson. Supper + early bed. . . .

November 15

Sunday— Went into the Elton for lunch with Rip and her family and Dot Dryden— Mr. Ripley perfectly darling—!—! Had the most delicious luncheon. Lobster Newburg etc—etc. Got a bunch of lilies of the valley + a red rose— After lunch we sat in the lobby and soon Elias and Polly Page came and Rip + I stood + talked to them for about a half-hour. Went home in a machine about 3.30. Had a *heavenly* time————!—!

November 30

Monday—1914— Birthday. 16 yr. had a birthday table of Bug, Midge—Caddy—Tommy—Gin Burus— + Rip—

December 25

Friday— [In Chicago.] Merry Christmas.—! Peg's for breakfast. Went home early. Trunk has come at last. Opened presents. All wonderful. Flowers from Dan—picture of John, and 5 lb. box of candy from B. Mitchell— John came + called in the aft. Family party for lunch of 15. No supper. Bath + bed early.

December 27

Sunday— Slept late—till 11:30. Breakfast at 12. + I went home at 12.30. Lunch at home and in the middle of it one of my two remaining baby teeth came out, much to my surprise.* Bill Mitchell came in Jack's Loco to take me for a ride at 3.15 and we went out to the park for a ride— He stayed a while afterwards at the house and after he had left Mother + I went to Aunt Lillian's for tea and stayed there till 6 o'clock— Early supper + bed—

January 1

1915 Happy New Year— Have an awful cold. Stayed in bed all morn. Felt rather rotten. Got up and went to Adelaide Pierce's breakfast, danced. Went home with Peg + had another light luncheon— Went to Burry's tea at Collins Studio for a while + then to the Casino for tea with Billy Odell, Kim Walsey, Pollock + Mr. + Mrs. Carry + Peg. Home to dress for dinner. Sanford Otis took me over. Sent me some sweet pease. Deering, Courtney, John + I sat together at supper. . . .

January 2

1915—Saturday— Spent night with Peg. Marie [Hersey] came on 8.45 train + she + Mother came over + got me. Went to old house, then to Lincoln Hall + then to new house till lunch.† Mrs. Spoors

---

* This was eight days before she met Scott.

† Ginevra's family was relocating from her Grandfather Fuller's house at 2913 Michigan Avenue to her parents' new house at Astor and Burton.

gave a lunch + matinee of Big F. . . . Went to "New Henrietta" afterwards. Pretty fair. Went home + got dressed for Charman's dinner. Punk. Billy Mitchell + Mr. + Mrs. Ripley sent me flowers. Big Four dance. Went swell. Stopped at 12. Gil darling— Home to new house + bed——!

January 3

Sunday— Slept late till 11.30 + had breakfast at 12. Went back to old house for lunch with Marie + family. After lunch Dudley, Midge + Gil called Bug + I up. Said goodbye. Dan McCarthy called— (Ha-Ha) Went to new house about 4.30 + Billy Odell + Dan came over to see us, + went at 5.45 for the train. Train left at 6.30 and we went in for dinner soon after— Champagne punch. Ha-ha again. Bed at 10. Read magazine + tried to sleep.

January 4

Monday— Arrived at St. Paul at 7.20. Edward met us at the train and we went to 475 Summit Ave. for breakfast. Saw Hamilton + Jack + Mrs. Hersey. Had a bath after breakfast and later on a shampoo downtown. Went to Smiths etc. Home for lunch. After lunch Reuben Warner, Bob Dunn, Larry Elias + Frank Hurley + I went to the Orpheum. Awfully funny. Came home in R's car. Adorable (both). Got dressed for dinner. Larry, Betty, Midge, Kit, Mary, Frank H., *Scott Fitz-Gerald*. Reuben, Jimmie Johnston, Bobbie Schirmer, Bill Lindsee. Sat between Scott + Reuben, danced for a while afterwards. Scott perfectly darling. Am dipped about.

January 5

Tuesday— Got a letter from Gil this morn. darling— Slept late + had breakfast in bed. Went over to Mrs. Backus school for a while with Lib McDavitt. Lunch. Reuben + Scott came over at 2 + we decided to go to Minneapolis in R's car. Sort of crowded. Am absolutely gone on Scott! Dressed for dinner. Afterwards Jimmie J. and F. Hurley came + got us + took us to Lib MacD. Danced and sat with Scott most all evening. He left for Princeton at 11—oh—! Went for ride in R's car with Bug and J.J. Fun. Home at 12———— Scott—!

January 6

Wednesday— Slept late + breakfasted in bed. Got dressed at 12 + went to Kitty Schultze's for lunch + afterwards to a "Pair of Sixes" with Mrs. Hersey, Miss Fuch, Reuben, Jimmie + Bug. Awfully good— Went to the University Club for tea with Kit Ordway + a bunch had tea + danced— Fun— Went home + got dressed for dinner— At 8.30 Bob Dunn + Jimmie J. came for us in a taxi. Went to movies + sat in box— Left for Ramalley's dance hall at 9.30 + danced there till Reuben came at 10.45— Got stuck on car tracks but finally got home— Bed————!

January 7

Thursday—Got a Special Delivery from *Scott* this morning— Slept late + had breakfast in bed. Got dressed at 12.30— Lunch— Bob Dunn + Reuben came over + we decided to go coasting at the country club. It wasn't much good so Bug + I tobogganed on the back of Reuben's car. Went back to Smith's for refreshments +

then home (the long way). Got dressed + sat around + read.
Supper. Left St. Paul on 8.40 train. Bob Dunn and R.W. came to
the station. B.D. sent flowers. Had a perfectly wonderful time—!
To bed early.

January 8

Friday. Arrived in Chicago at 9. Went to Marshall F's + bought.
Go to dentist 10 till 12—oculist till 1— Lunch at Blackstone with
Mother. Went to Thomas Orchestra concert til 4 + then to
"Submarine Expedition" in movies at Fine Arts Theatre with
Edith, Dec. + Mrs. Dexter + Mrs. Cummings. Awfully good.
Home to new house. Dressed + then went to see children at old
house. Supper at Aunt Lillians. Nothing but sit around afterwards.
Home, bath + bed at 10—

January 15

Friday—1915— [Ginevra is back at Westover.] Sleepover—
Stayed in my room till recess + then into inf[irmary]. In with Ann
Meirs + Jennie Martin. Wrote letters— Read Kipling + talked to
Courtney— Wonderful letter from Scott again to-day! Reuben
sent me a five pound box of Smith's candy way from St. Paul. Bob
Dunn sent Bug some.

January 18

Monday—1915— Glee Club at 9.15. Long talk with Court + Peg
in my room. Made Big Four constitution and discussed *various*
topics. Lunch. Played cards with Sal + Tommy in T's room all aft.

Rip came back before study-hour. Glad to see her— Letters from Gil, *Scott,* Martha G. and Mother. Rip sat by me at supper. Chapel with Rip + Peg. Permish to talk.

January 25

Monday—1915. Left infirmary about 4 in the aft. Emma left in the morning. . . . Wrote 5 more letters. Got letters from Reuben + Nathan. From Betty at night. Fatherly lecture. Had a talk with Bug about it + other things. Came to the conclusion that I am pretty much of a fool + simply *have* to be careful———! Bed + talked with Rip about the same thing.

January 29

Friday—1915— *Holiday*— Lecture on District house by Mr. Lewis + Miss MacQuaid. . . . Mary R. suggested changing vac. till April 4— Vote taken at lunch—*not* changed. Wrote 20 page letter to Scott. Cake sale at Tea bureau* in aft. . . . Supper—(by Violet). Danced in gym. Slept with Bug. Rip was sore— Letter from Elias, Nathan—Mother

February 22

Monday. Tom, Sal + I went for a long walk this A.M. Wonderful spring day. Watched cows etc. etc. Played 500 all aft. Went to Washington's birthday carnival in gym. Great. Peanuts, lollipops +

---

* Tea was served at Westover in the afternoons at the "tea bureau."

bum lemonade— How I wish I was either up at Hotchkiss, Woodstock or Taft— Te-dum. No avail.*

March 10

Wednesday 1915— Still in infirmary. Read "Pendennis" (some of it) and knitted. Am thrilled to death about going home and simply *cant* wait to get away from this dirty hole and see the family, all my friends and the new house!!!!! Came out in aft. Concert by singing class in Room 20— About 20 people there— 5 letters to-day— Pretty good. Exced from chapel. Read Bug's old letters from Scott and some of mine.

March 17

Wednesday—1915— Got *HOME*. The new house is simply *too* beautiful for words— My room is *divine!* As is the whole house. Got a new bonnet + shoes + had a great swim with Mother at the Athletic Club in morn. Home for lunch. Dr. Schmidt, Miss Buckley here in aft. Went to Mary's dancing class, saw Rus, Kieth, Ralph, H. Clausen, Dick Pope. Billy K. Billy O. Deering called me up + Wallie Lo. called. Early supper— Bath + Bed—*Lord, I am tired.*

March 20

Saturday 1915. Dancing lesson for me at 10.15. Miss Buckley's. Shopped til 12.15— Home— Deering came for lunch. Went with

---

* Nearby boys' prep schools.

Mother to see D. Warfield in the "Auctioneer" afterwards. Great—
Came home + got dressed for Harriet for supper— Lolita, Lila,
Edie, Kieth, Rus + Channon + I were there. Afterwards Rus + I
gave each other a dancing lesson. Then to the Parker for the
dance— *It was great!* Billy Odell, B. Kelley, Deering, Dan, Cully,
Wallie, Rus were all too wonderful— Deering esp. I'm simply
gone on anything to do with dancing. D.D. certainly can dance—!
Pa + Ma took Rus and I home— Bed + sore feet—

April 1

Thursday—1915. [Back at Westover.] School in morn. *Marks* were
read. Mine was 88, and I *didn't* get a conduct mark, thank heaven.
Danced in the aft. for the pantomime + then walked with Edith.
Letter from *Scott*. Great. Danced in gym with Peg. Chapel with
Kate. Slept with E.— + Peg + we laughed + talked till all hours.

April 15

Thursday— School— *Tennis began!* Practised songs all aft. At
night Pep, Dot Dudley, B. Norman, Midge, Scheff, Tuttie + I went
over to the church + sang— *Fine* supper— Great fun. Slept with
Midge. Talked till all hours.

April 29

Thursday. School in morn. Played b.b. in afternoon. Awful! Then
tournament (tennis) with Gin against Minna + Peg Tuttle. Got
beaten 6–1, 7–5— Rotten! Exed from part of study hour to take

bath. Started + almost finished Scarlet Letter in study hall. Glee
Club, then Midge's birthday table. Sat next to Midge + Livie—
Mr. Souret lectured. With Bug (only she didn't come).

M a y 7

1915. Friday— Exed from all periods in school— School.
Decorated gym—in aft. *Lusitania reported to have been sunk off*
Queenstown by German Torpedo boat. Stevens family and Miss Pope
on it!!—!* Chapel with Rip + Rem.

J u n e 2

Wednesday—1915— *Marks* in morn. Mine—88.6— 1 conduct
mark *again*. Holiday afterwards—(Miss Pope's). Played hockey—
Cards in aft. till Lantern picnic— Wonderful—same as last year—
cold as the deuce—went with Tom, Bug + Sal— Got home and
found some mignon roses from Midge + orchids from Bug— Bath
+ bed.

---

* Theodate Pope, the second-in-command at Westover, was a passenger on the
Lusitania; she escaped in a lifeboat.

FIVE LETTERS FROM GINEVRA

(January 20 1915)

> *Westover,*
> *Middlebury, Conn.*
> *Wednesday.*

(I'm not the artistic or poetic type or I'd do some
  Michael Angelo's and Van Dyke's on my letters too!)

Dear Scott——:
    This is a <u>very</u> serious letter so for goodness sakes, <u>don't</u> read
it until you feel in that sort of a mood——!
    I'm <u>terribly</u> sorry you don't think I was sincere when I said I
enjoyed your letters. They <u>don't</u> only "amuse me"——for I like
them so much because——well, just because they <u>are</u> so nice! If
you don't believe me when I say I never read such interesting
ones, <u>what</u> can I do?
    Am I supposed to take the fact that I'm fading from your

*memory as a compliment or otherwise— I suppose there's so
little to me that I'm not hard to forget quickly—*

Really, though, even if this is *the case I have enough pride
not to want you to say I am a speed or anything like that— Do
you honestly think I am? Answer please—(truth!)*

Now Scott this is heart to heart and therefore private!

*A few years ago I took pleasure in being called "fast" (if
that were possible [at] as young an age as 13 or 14) But
anyway, I didn't care how I acted, I liked it, and so I didn't
care for what people said— Naturally this was crazy, but I was
young, I'm only sixteen now and that isn't aged—*

*About a year ago I began to see that there was something
better in life than what I had been doing, and I honestly tried to
act properly, but I am afraid I'll never be able to wholly reform
as to the extent of being an angel!*

*I know I am a flirt and I can't stop it. I really haven't got
such a "line" as everyone thinks for I mean a lot of what I say
way down deep and nobody ever believes me. Except for this, I
am pretty good on the whole, but you know how much alike we
are, and in a boy it doesn't matter, but a girl has to control her
feelings, which is hard for me, as I am emotional.*

*The inner workings of my mind would or would not be of
interest to you, as the case may be— But I do think a lot
though, more than people think I do, although I haven't very
much sense. I have more than some people credit me with I
hope, only I don't know how to use it. I know you think I'm a
perfect fool, but really I wish you wouldn't think so, as, though
I did flirt with you, I really like you a lot.*

*I have never written to anyone such a letter as this, but if we
don't ever see each other again it's the only way we'd ever get to*

know each other. I wish you'd write me a letter and tell me the same thing, just how much of a fool you think I am, and for Mercy's sakes! <u>Be Frank!</u>

After all this that I've written you, I trust you will tell me as much of the truth as I've told you. And I hope I haven't bored you to tears!

Take every word of this as the perfect truth, on my word of honor—

This is the kind of letter you said you wanted, and so this is what I wrote. I'm still petrified over exams. I wish you better luck than I'll have on mine— Write soon and say that you understand

Yours Ginevra.

P.S. That was the <u>most</u> impossible dream! I hope you don't think it characteristic. G.K.

P.P.S. I don't know what you meant by "tell me what the Big Four did— I think it's a fake!" Answer this surely.

(January 25 1915)

Sunday
Westover,
Middlebury, Conn.

Well, Scott F. Fitzgerald, you ought to be thankful and grateful that I wrote seven other letters before I wrote you! I'll tell you why! Principally because I've let off all my steam about coming exams, the weather, lack of pep and so forth, and am free and ready to write you a more interesting letter. I suppose a letter isn't complete without a "dear" in it, so here goes—

Dear—; Why repeat the Scott? It is understood. Your last letter was a marvel—I howled over it and wept over it by turns! I did in truth! I see you dont believe me. Well, to tell you the truth, I was pleased beyond words to get a <u>frank</u> letter from you! Also I was pleased at <u>some</u> of the things you said, but the others, <u>no!!</u>

"Jamais de la vie" That remark about the "Confessions of a V." was entirely uncalled for and I hope to goodness you don't think <u>that</u> of me.

Also when you said I hadn't any character. I consider that a personal insult— I must be a fine kind of a girl— No sense, no character, a flirt! Still, I might as well take my medicine, as I asked you what I <u>was and that is what I am</u>— No! And a 100 times NO! Of course Reuben didn't kiss me at the station <u>or anywhere else!</u> No fears on that score—! I think him very nice and attractive and cute—and yes, I've gotten two letters from him, also a wonderful box of Smith's candy that the poor boy blew himself to, but which I never even saw as it is not allowed here, and was carted off to a boy's club in Waterbury— What do you mean by this Scott? "They say you have some comeback" Also, I did not understand what you meant by asking me why I laughed when you gave me your "Mouchoir" at the MacDavitt's— The reason that I laughed was that I was embarrassed.

(I hope the fact that I never write over 4 pages to anybody else is appreciated)

Why my picture doesn't come is a mystery to me too, I am sure. It ought to have been here long ago. And oh Scott another thing—what did you mean by "Who is this Mitchell" I cant imagine—Mitchell what? Mitchell Tires!* So? (This is my new expression, to get everybody's goat) Also, in one place you insinuated that I did not mean it when I said I really liked you an awful lot. Here is an argument for you, if you like me, and we are both so much alike in every respect, <u>why</u> shouldn't <u>I like you</u>, too? Really, Scott I wish you'd believe me—! I don't know why, but I must be awfully drawn to you, for the minute I start to write to you I have a hundred and one things to say, whereas everybody else, I can only think up enough to say for four pages. But to go on— Scott, I'm surprised! I hear you had plans for kissing me goodbye publicly. My goodness, I'm glad you didn't— I'd have had to be severe as anything with you! <u>Ans. this—Why didn't you? (KISS ME)</u>

Oh, the funniest thing happened last night! A boy from Hotchkiss called John Hamline called me up on the telephone and I didn't recognize his voice— It sounded a lot like yours. He said, "I met you in St. Paul, <u>don't</u> you know who <u>I</u> am?" I didn't want to seem like a bone, so I said,— "Is—this— Scott?" Then he said, "Well I caught you then" and proceeded to tease the life out of me. I read a letter from Betty Mudge to Bug last night and she had heard from Ed Powers that Dan was furiously jealous at me! His tart letters sound like it. Really they are jokes— I have written him two very stinging ones this week (just finished one of them) just for the joy of stinging him, and he has written me three equally horrid so at present we're

---

* This is Bill Mitchell, whom Ginevra would marry in 1918.

not on very <u>affable</u> terms— Edie P. called Bug up last night on the telephone and they talked for almost an hour, so long that at last they were <u>told</u> they had to stop— She also got such a long letter from him last night that it had to be put in 2 envelopes! Talk about being "en amour" "C'est pas au meme classe" (you see, I have been studying for a French exam.)

You know Scott, that before I started out to write you, I didn't have any idea I could write such a long letter and not begin to complain about the weather, the exams and my awful cold—! Aren't you honored though?

Let me think, is there anything else I had to tell you. Oh— I had a dream about you the other night, but I'd never tell you what it was about, only that you did the rescuing act— I have been reading the part of your letter where you said something about "The same sort of girl" and have fallen into [a] somewhat sentimental state. I wish a girl could write a sentimental letter and not be criticized— I also wish that I would at the present moment get a long wonderful letter from you— "Distance lends enchantment" Oh I feel so mushy tonight, I'm glad I didn't feel this way in St. Paul, I wish we were riding home from Minneapolis now. Oh, how I wish it, Scott. I'm going to stay in this mood, thinking of my second aft. in St. Paul, till tomorrow morning and <u>then to work</u> till Thursday evening when exams are over and then—oh joy— And Scott, <u>please</u> dont think I forgot you when you went away. I was thinking of you the whole time—well—I think I better stop. I am so proud of the length of this that I have been waving it around taking it all in and I hate to pack it into a tight wad again! (Sort of nobody at home)

I hope to <u>goodness</u> you appreciate its length and begin to

realize that I've <u>never</u> written such a letter before in all my days.
<u>Do</u> write soon—and long— I am

your Ginevra.

P.S. Just reread this, excuse the last page.

(Please scan)

P.S. Notice the paper—it is new! Also homely, also it is my
excuse for writing you so soon again.

(March 25 1915)

[From Chicago.]
Wednesday eve.
at 9.52 P.M.
au lit—

Dear Scott—

I've just bade a fond farewell to two youths who leave on the
10:30 train for California. They're going in a private car and
are going to stay only two weeks in all— Isn't that crazy? Isn't
it funny, when I got your letter, I was talking on the telephone
and so I said "Just wait a minute, I'll open this letter, so I can
read while you're talking." And then the first words on the page
were "Even now you may be having a tete-a-tete with some
'unknown Chicagoan' with crisp dark hair and glittering
smile." Well you'd appreciate the coincidence. You say

Deering. He's the darkest thing I ever set eyes on and <u>has</u> a glittering smile. I read him that passage of the letter, as it was so appropriate. But Scott, if I could only believe that you didn't mean all you said in that letter!

I'm terribly terribly horribly afraid that it's a case of plain tiredness, if there is such a word, on <u>your</u> part, I mean— You needn't worry about me. Of course you think that because I'm here with a lot of boys, I have forgotten you, but I know it'll make me like you all the better, because you see, all last term I didn't think of a thing but <u>you</u>—(this is as sincere as I've <u>ever</u> been) and by the end of the term naturally my mental powers had given out, and a rest was just what I needed. There are some peachy boys here now.

The Winters, the Kelleys and numerous others, and I am practically the <u>only</u> girl, consequently I'm simply having a glorious time. There have been one or two boys over every night and in the afternoon we go to the thé dansants at the Blackstone, or else they come and call or we fool around somehow— It is a lot more formal here than in St. Paul, but I suppose that's because this is a bigger city. It is <u>some baby city though</u> and I'm mad about it and everything belonging to it. What is your add. during vacation or would you rather <u>not</u> have me write?

That French phrase <u>was</u> sort of peculiar— I'm sorry. I dont know what I meant, but I think probably—"Il n'y a pas pour l'emprendre"— Meaning mon coeur—boger! Let's see, were there any more questions. I don't think so.

Isn't it awful the way writers slander my name—? You've read the "Bride of Mistletoe" haven't you? Her name was Ginevra and Shelly or Keats wrote a horrible one about a

Ginevra too. * *They always seem to have something perfectly dreadful happen to them on their wedding day— That will be my fate I guess, my husband will probably run away——! — And I don't wonder—*

Your letter showed just exactly what you thought of me, and if I hadn't heard of your plan to pick a quarrel it would have started one in a second, with out a doubt. As it was, I was terribly disappointed to think that you thought <u>that</u> badly of me and moreover, I dont think personally that I'm as bad as you intimated.

Your view is ridiculous— Just because you and I—for we are remarkably alike—just because you and I happen to be "fresh" (excuse me) and have more emotional feeling than most other people have, we're bound, simply <u>bound</u> to let it out some way, sometime: and nothing under the sun could control our feelings— They're bound to show themselves— You know you cant <u>help</u> falling madly for a girl. It isn't really <u>you</u> yourself that does it, it's an indescribable thing inside of you— Of course that's somewhat what makes you fascinating. I'm perfectly fascinated with some boys I'm willing to admit, especially ones whose reps. are in bad condition, and who I oughtn't to pay any attention to. (Of course this is not personal. <u>Dont</u> think so Please.) That's the reason I'm going to marry some awful reckless fellow, just for the sake of the excitement and that I would want to help him reform. This is a childish view, you may think, but its <u>my</u> view. I'd marry any kind of a man under the sun— "Richman, poorman, beggarman, thief," etc., if I really loved him.

---

* See Appendix 5, "Other Ginevras."

I know you cant mistake true love—I know it. And it's a sin not to recognize it. Although of course an outrageous thing to go completely against the wishes of your family. There are loads and loads of boys here of course, but I don't think that there's one to marry. The bunch we go with, are really what you might call "speeds" or at least some of them, and although I presume they are rather a bad influence it gives a girl a great experience in loads of things (I can hear you say "Gee whiz—! she hasn't any experience—!")

I defy you, Scott Fitzgerald! I have love in me—Nothing could hurt me more than you have to say that—

"Never have anybody really love you!" Well that is probably very true, but if the right man does come along, I'll have love to give him. If nothing else in this world—(at least, I think so)

You show your ignorance of my nature well by saying that I haven't ever really loved anybody. Naturally I'm awfully, awfully young, but there have been times in my life, in the last few years, where I felt something deeper and truer and more sincere than mere shallow affection. You see, I've done a lot more for my age than almost any girl, especially those in the East.

You're crazy! You dont mean to tell me that you dont think that [a] girl who, when young, is a flirt, will ever get her share of life. Why, those sort of women almost invariably make the best wives—

"Eat, drink and be merry for tomorrow we die," may be some people's attitude to-wards life, and I can see their view but there's something more than that to be gotten from it. (That sounded just like Church on Sunday)

Heavens! I dont mean to preach for I'm far, far from anything like that. You probably dont think I ever think of anything more

than a good time, and being crazy about some boy, and loads of
other people dont think so either, but there's where you're wrong,
Scott, and though there probably isn't a bit of anything that's
"worth while" in me, I want you to see the way I _really_ feel. I
managed to read what you said about letting you go, as you weren't
wasting affections on [blank space]. Well, if I hadn't wanted to
use more than those ordinary "affections" on you, I'd have stopped
long ago. And then, something drew me to you, I don't know
why— It just—did. It must have, or else I wouldn't be writing you
this or anything else of the truck you've gotten from me.

    You are conceited, I'll have to admit that. No reason why
you shouldn't be and then, I'm vain, (and self-conscious, some
people say, of my self-confidence) That's another thing, I am as
un-self-confident as any mortal ever was, yet some say I'm very
self conscious of my self confidence.

    Poor Scott, I guess you're bored enough— I'm terribly sorry
about your not being able to come to see me at my aunts, as I'd
give some anything to see you, but suppose it can't be did. After
Monday morn. my address is at school—! oho—!

    Please Scott understand this letter and I know you wont
think I'm such a fool.

> Write soon—
> With love,
> Ginevra.

    P.S. It is now 11:05 P.M. Yet I met G. McIlvaine. Doesn't
he remember me— Big stiff— Strange—Huh.

    P.S. Notice the length of this also writing. G. K. You must
be in a _very serious mood_ for this. G.

(April 19, 1915)

Sunday

Dear S——

I'm overjoyed to see that you understood about the dance and everything.* It makes me more—more blue every time I think of it, and I dont [know] <u>what</u> we're going to do, if we only see each other that one night—June 8th. My goodness, if you dont pay a darn lot of attention to me and no other, that night, why—I don't know <u>what</u> will happen— I told Edith Cummings that Mother had said she couldn't chaperone me this spring, and she said in a nonchalant way "Oh come along with me, Mother will chaperone us both"— She didn't sound enthused so I let the subject drop, but the dear girl didn't realize what she had said. Anyway, I'd already written you about it— I don't quite see how she can be going with her cousin, who is a <u>Senior</u>! Do you——??—

I only have a minute to write so excuse this if it's only a note— Yes, I certainly <u>do</u> save letters! I wouldn't throw yours away for the world, and have them at present locked up in my strong-box—only there are so many that they dont all quite go in! Every now and then, when I feel blue, I pull out a nice long, fat one, and read it through. We'll have that party some day soon, only I wont burn your letters, and I <u>wont</u> have you read mine out loud, they're too absurd——! I often wonder if they sound simply killing when read by some other person, but you see when I write to you, I always feel just as though I was talking

---

* Ginevra has told Scott that she cannot come to the prom.

to you, and as I say foolish things sometimes, I am just as liable to write them in my letters— I know, if I ever saw one of my letters again, I would think myself crazy. That's the reason I felt so foolish when I got that slang letter. I read it to a girl here, Virginia Burns, Portland—Oregon, who uses more slang than anyone I know (she met Mr. Jackson (excuse change of ink) in Easter vac.) She thought it was just lovely and Bug has been asking to see it ever since! You asked if Darrow Fulton stayed over a week from college to amuse me! Well, it was "comme ca"—he had to get off a condition at a tutoring school before entering Yale last fall, and he just stayed over a week longer at Pittsfield, where I was— C' est tout—! Not very thrilling!

How is the Triangle show getting on?

May I not give you some "helping Hints"— Come down and teach the chorus or something like that—? I'm sure I would do an awful lot of good—

Scott! Did I honestly use all these slang words in my letters. For heavens sakes go through them again and cross out all of them. I dont suppose that would leave much reading-matter though— I intended to write you a very sensible beautifully worded epistle, but it took much too much bean and time and besides it didn't sound a bit natural.

Last night the Seniors gave a dance, the only time in the year when Males are allowed to roam around the place. I played tennis all afternoon to try and get a slant at them, and succeeded pretty well, but there were only two or three that I knew— I spent most of the night lying on a pillow by the window, watching the dancing and listening to the music— It was so divine— "Oh Tennessee—I hear you calling me"——
Oh——

"I didn't raise my boy to be a soldier"— Both are too cute for words I think—!

Scott, you contradicted yourself in the last-but-one letter. Firstly, do you remember that when you came up here, it was a marvelous day, and you said that fine days always depressed you— well— secondly— in your last letter, you said "on rainy days I wake up and immediately begin to gloom—but spring days and fine weather make me happy and excited and peppy." Which do you mean (N.B.) Be _sure_ and answer this, as it is of _vital_ importance—!!!! You understand, I suppose, that my life depends on it— Oh yes— oh yes—!

I agree with you though, that life in the sunshine is very bright, and at this rate and with this weather, I ought to be the peppiest little thing going! Tennis and Basketball have been going on all week and I am [a] shark in both sports, _of course_— Oh Lordy! My game of tennis is pitiful—! Let's see, I had loads to tell you, but cant think of anything now as the bell is ringing and I must away————

Yours "Comme et pour toujours!"
Ginevra.

(Jan. 31, 1916.)

Dear Scott—

Just so as to not disappoint you I am writing this the day after I got your letter. In fact, I got it last night and am answering it immediately (Sunday morn) It may be long and it may be short. That depends entirely on the mood in which I finish it.

*Exams start on Tuesday and naturally I ought to be
studying for them now, but as it is, I haven't cracked a book!
However, I dont expect to pass so am not worried in the least!
Got a bid to a tea dance from Joe Shanley the other day for Feb.
19th to meet the Triangle and regretted it with <u>much</u> gloom—
How I hate to get bids that I know I cant go to, and that I want
to go to so badly— Why were schools ever invented anyway.*

*My, but that must have been stupid to read over my old
letters. After you finished them, you must have thought me the
greatest fool in the world. However, you must admit that your
letters were much more interesting. Some of them I even know
by heart.*

*You carried off what you told me about— (You know, the
night before the Y-P game) wonderfully, and I'm certain that
no-one suspected it at all— I know I didn't, but I'm afraid that
the whole evening must have been an awful bore to you.*

*Midge wants to know why you told Kirkland Jones that she
was "the worst." Ans. Caddy is dictating the following to me—
"To tell you that she invites me to visit her anytime during
August when you will be with Sam"— She wont be there in
July!— Isn't that divine, as the four of us ought to be able to
have some awfully good parties! Honestly and truly, it would
be wonderful to have that perfect hour, sometime, someday and
somewhere. I really think that it would be divine and I think we
might be able to find something to talk about. Anyway we've got
to arrange it next summer. I have a sneaky feeling that you
wouldn't speak to me by the time that the week is up, because
you would be so bored with me. Your last letter was divine
though, and it seemed like old times to be getting such a nice
long one from you—*

Early this morning I felt just like writing you a heart-to-heart letter, and all thro' chapel I thought out what I was going to say to you, but somehow I have forgotten it now, worse luck—

The last part of your letter was the truest thing I have ever read, and so exactly fitted in with my ideas on such subjects, that it was almost amusing! You seem to feel the same way that I do about being crazy about people, and I suppose it's just human nature to want to own things, only a girl, I think, would rather belong to somebody she loved, more than wanting to own him— Of course I suppose that includes having the person belong to you, so that isn't any argument. Why oh why isn't it possible for us to have at least one long talk absolutely alone. We certainly have enough in common and would get to know each other about 100% better if we only could— But no, the inevitable chap is always on the scene!!! Do you know I often wonder why my ideas about some things dont coincide with any other girls—or at least, not many others. Bug is about the only one I can think of now— Court and I certainly clash in our views sometimes. If I had my way everything would be a lot freer, do you see what I mean— Not so darn much convention etc. and everybody would be able to say exactly what they pleased, and not be any the worse for it. But if "wishes were horses, all beggars would ride." And most people are tied down pretty darn tight by the conventional "What will People say." Seems to me no matter what a person does, if they themselves think they are in the right, there isn't a reason in the world for worrying about what the other person will say. Perhaps you dont agree, but I feel this way. I'm telling you about it. I feel exactly the same way towards you as you say you do to me. No matter if I do ever get crazy about anyone else, I'll always sort of feel that I know you best, or at least better than most boys, even if I *have* only *seen* you a few times, and I know that I can always come to you and talk to you and you'll cheer me up if I get down and out. (this sounds as though I was making my last will and testament, but it isn't meant that way) The worst of it is, that you *dont* want to know me, and I *do* want to know you, 'cause it's no use having me on a pedestal if I have no business being there!— I don't see why Midge should have objected to your remark, about feeling that you could get what you want, because confidence (not an over-amount, of course) but self-confidence is a wonderful thing and its hard luck not to have any. Perhaps it is because Midge has none that she didn't like the remark— I'd give anything in the world for a little!!! Anyone can get so much farther and so much more out of life if they have a little.

No, I dont think passion would have made you kiss me on the porch and in our house that day, because I pride myself enough to say that it would have been "nerve" and nerve alone that would have made you do it— I may be wrong— Tell me if I am!—

I would so much rather have you take me in a more friendly (no, not that exactly) way, instead of idealizing me, because honestly and truly, Scott, I'm not worth it! It's no use your ever thinking so, and by admitting that I probably have made you lose all interest in me whatsoever—

If you understand at all what I'm trying to write, answer me and tell me if you do—

Hope you had a great time at Princeton——— and just you buck up and *make* yourself think you're getting well, and the

first think you know—you'll be fine again— Anyway, dont
forget I'm praying for you——*
    Wish me luck in my exams, and appreciate my long
letter——

                                        Yours with love,
                                        Ginevra

---

* Fitzgerald was home in St. Paul, having temporarily withdrawn from Princeton
because of failing grades and poor health.

"*BABES IN THE WOODS*"

Scott published "Babes in the Woods" in the May 1917 issue of the *Nassau Literary Magazine*. In the story he merges incidents from two parties held in St. Paul in January 1915. The first, at which he met Ginevra, was at Marie Hersey's house on Monday, January 4th; the second was at Lib McDavitt's house the following evening. He borrowed the title of the story from the song "Babes in the Wood" by Jerome Kern and Schuyler Greene; this was a brother-sister duet in the 1915 Broadway musical *Very Good Eddie*. Lyrics from the song appear toward the end of the story. Scott revised "Babes" and republished it in the *Smart Set* for September 1919. He also used the story in Book I, Chapter 2, of *This Side of Paradise*. The text reprinted here is from the *Nassau Lit* appearance.

BABES IN THE WOODS

I.

At the top of the stairs she paused. The emotions of divers on spring-boards, leading-ladies on opening nights, and lumpy, be-striped young men on the day of the Big Game, crowded through her. She felt as if she should have descended to a burst of drums or to a discordant blend of gems from Thaïs and Carmen. She had never been so worried about her appearance, she had never been so satisfied with it. She had been sixteen years old for two months.

"Isabelle!" called Elaine from her doorway.

"I'm ready," she caught a slight lump of nervousness in her throat.

"I've got on the wrong slippers and stockings—you'll have to wait a minute."

Isabelle started toward Elaine's door for a last peek at a mirror, but something decided her to stand there and gaze down the stairs. They curved tantalizingly and she could just catch a glimpse of two pairs of masculine feet in the hall below. Pump-shod in uniform black they gave no hint of identity, but eagerly she wondered if one pair were attached to Kenneth Powers. This young man, as yet unmet, had taken up a considerable part of her day—the first day of her arrival. Going up in the machine from the station Elaine had volunteered, amid a rain of questions and comment, revelation and exaggeration—

"Kenneth Powers is simply *mad* to meet you. He's stayed over a day from college and he's coming to-night. He's heard so much about you—"

It had pleased her to know this. It put them on more equal terms, although she was accustomed to stage her own romances with or without a send-off. But following her delighted tremble of anticipation came a sinking sensation which made her ask:

"How do you mean he's heard about me? What sort of things?"

Elaine smiled—she felt more or less in the capacity of a showman with her more exotic guest.

"He knows you're good looking and all that." She paused— "I guess he knows you've been kissed."

Isabelle had shuddered a bit under the fur robe. She was accustomed to be followed by this, but it never failed to arouse in her the same feeling of resentment; yet—in a strange town it was an advantage. She was a speed, was she? Well? Let them find out. She wasn't quite old enough to be sorry nor nearly old enough to be glad.

"Anne (this was another schoolmate) told him, I didn't—I knew you wouldn't like it," Elaine had gone on naively. "She's coming over to-night to the dinner."

Out the window Isabelle watched the high-piled snow glide by in the frosty morning. It was ever so much colder here than in Pittsburg; the glass of the side door was iced and the windows were shirred with snow in the corners. Her mind played still with the one subject. Did he dress like that boy there who walked calmly down what was evidently a bustling business street, in moccasins and winter-carnival costume? How very *western!* Of course he wasn't that way: he went to college, was a freshman or something. Really she had no distinct idea of him. A two year back picture had not impressed her except by the big eyes, which he had probably grown up to by now. However in the last two weeks at school, when her Christmas visit to Elaine had been decided on, he had assumed the proportions of a worthy adversary. Children, the most astute of matchmakers, plot and plan quickly and Elaine had cleverly played a word sonata to Isabelle's excitable temperament. Isabelle was and had been for some time capable of very strong, if not very transient emotions.

They drew up at a spreading red stone building, set back from the snowy street. Mrs. Terrell greeted her rather impersonally and Elaine's various younger brothers were produced from the corners where they skulked politely. Isabelle shook hands most tactfully. At her best she allied all with whom she came in contact, except older girls and some women. All the impressions that she made were conscious. The half dozen girls she met that morning were all rather impressed—and as much by her direct personality as by her reputation. Kenneth Powers seemed an unembarrassed subject of conversation. Evidently he was a bit light of love. He was neither popular nor unpopular. Every girl there seemed to have had an affair with him at some time or other, but no one volunteered any really useful information. He was going to fall for her. Elaine had issued that statement to her young set and they were retailing it back to Elaine as fast as they set eyes on Isabelle. Isabelle resolved mentally, that if necessary, she would force herself to like him—she owed it to Elaine. What if she were terribly disappointed. Elaine had painted him in such glowing colors—he was good looking, had a "line" and was properly inconstant. In fact he summed up all the romance that her age and environment led her to desire. Were those his dancing shoes that fox-trotted tentatively around the soft rug below?

All impressions and in fact all ideas were terribly kaleidoscopic to Isabelle. She had that curious mixture of the social and artistic temperaments, found often in two classes, society women and actors. Her education, or rather her sophistication, had been absorbed from the boys who had dangled upon her favor, her tact was instinctive and her capacity for love affairs was limited only by the number of boys she met. Flirt smiled from her large, black-brown eyes and figured in her intense physical magnetism.

So she waited at the head of the stairs that evening while slippers and stockings were changed. Just as she was getting impatient Elaine came out beaming with her accustomed good nature and high spirits. Together they descended the broad stairs while the nervous searchlight of Isabelle's mind flashed on two ideas. She was glad she had high color to-night and she wondered if he danced well.

Downstairs the girls she had met in the afternoon surrounded her for a moment, looking unbelievably changed by the soft yellow light; then she heard Elaine's voice repeating a cycle of names and she found herself bowing to a sextet of black and white and terribly stiff figures. The name Powers figured somewhere, but she did not place him at first. A confused and very juvenile moment of awkward backings and bumpings, and everyone found themselves arranged talking to the very persons they least desired to. Isabelle maneuvered herself and Peter Carroll, a sixth-former from Hotchkiss whom she had met that afternoon, to a seat at the piano. A reference, supposedly humorous, to the afternoon, was all she needed. What Isabelle could do socially with one idea was remarkable. First she repeated it rapturously in an enthusiastic contralto;

then she held it off at a distance and smiled at it—her wonderful smile; then she delivered it in variations and played a sort of mental catch with it, all this in the nominal form of dialogue. Peter was fascinated and totally unconscious that this was being done not for him but for the black eyes that glistened under the shining, carefully watered hair a little to her left. As an actor even in the fullest flush of his own conscious magnetism gets a lasting impression of most of the people in the front row, so Isabelle sized up Kenneth Powers. First, he was of middle height, and from her feeling of disappointment, she knew that she had expected him to be tall and of Vernon Castle-ish slenderness. His hair and eyes were his most noticeable possessions—they were black and they fairly glittered. For the rest, he had rather dark skin with a faint flush, and a straight romantic profile, the effect set off by a close-fitting dress suit and a silk ruffled shirt of the kind that women still delight in on men, but men were just beginning to get tired of.

Kenneth was just quietly smiling.

"Don't *you* think so?" she said suddenly, turning to him innocent eyed.

There was a stir near the door and Elaine led the way to dinner. Kenneth struggled to her side and whispered:

"You're my dinner partner—Isabelle."

Isabelle gasped—this was rather quick work. Of course it made it more interesting, but really she felt as if a good line had been taken from the star and given to a minor character. She mustn't lose the leadership a bit. The dinner table glittered with laughter at the confusion of getting places and then curious eyes were turned on her, sitting near the head. She was enjoying this immensely, and Peter Carroll was so engrossed with the added sparkle of her rising color that he forgot to pull out Elaine's chair and fell into a dim confusion.

Kenneth was on the other side, full of confidence and vanity, looking at her most consciously. He started directly and so did Peter.

"I've heard a lot about you——"

"Wasn't it funny this afternoon——"

Both stopped. Isabelle turned to Kenneth shyly. Her face was always enough answer for anyone, but she decided to speak.

"How—who from?"

"From everybody—for years." She blushed appropriately. On her right Peter was hors-de-combat already, although he hadn't quite realized it.

"I'll tell you what I thought about you when I first saw you," Kenneth continued. She leaned slightly toward him and looked modestly at the celery before her. Peter sighed—he knew Kenneth and the situations that Kenneth was born to handle. He turned to Elaine and asked her when she was going back to school.

II.

Isabelle and Kenneth were distinctly not innocent, nor were they particularly hardened. Moreover, amateur standing had very little value in the game they were beginning to play. They were simply very sophisticated, very calculating and finished, young actors, each playing a part that they had played for years. They had both started with good looks and excitable temperaments and the rest was the result of certain accessible popular novels, and dressing-room conversation culled from a slightly older set. When Isabelle's eyes, wide and innocent, proclaimed the ingenue most, Kenneth was proportionally less deceived. He waited for the mask to drop off, but at the same time he did not question her right to wear it. She, on her part, was not impressed by his studied air of blasé sophistication. She came from a larger city and had slightly an advantage in range. But she accepted his pose. It was one of the dozen little conventions of this kind of affair. He was aware that he was getting this particular favor now because she had been coached. He knew that he stood for merely the best thing in sight, and that he would have to improve his opportunity before he lost his advantage. So they proceeded, with an infinite guile that would have horrified the parents of both.

After dinner the party swelled to forty and there was dancing in a large ex-play-room downstairs. Everything went smoothly—boys cut in on Isabelle every few feet and then squabbled in the corners with: "You might let me get more than an *inch*," and "She didn't like it either—she told me so next time I cut in." It was true—she told everyone so, and gave every hand a parting pressure that said "You know that your dances are *making* my evening."

But time passed, two hours of it and the less subtle beaux had better learned to focus their pseudo-passionate glances elsewhere for eleven o'clock found Isabelle and Kenneth on a leather lounge in a little den off the music-room. She was conscious that they were a handsome pair and seemed to belong distinctively on this leather lounge while lesser lights fluttered and chattered down stairs. Boys who passed the door looked in enviously—girls who passed only laughed and frowned, and grew wise within themselves.

They had now reached a very definite stage. They had traded ages, eighteen and sixteen. She had listened to much that she had heard before. He was a freshman at college, sang in the glee club and expected to make the freshman hockey-team. He had learned that some of the boys she went with in Pittsburg were "terrible speeds" and came to parties intoxicated—most of them were nineteen or so, and drove alluring Stutzes. A good half of them seemed to have already flunked out of various boarding schools and colleges, but some of them bore good collegiate names that made him feel rather young. As a matter of fact Isabelle's acquaintance with college boys was mostly through older cousins. She had bowing acquaintance with a lot of young men who thought she was "a pretty kid" and "worth keeping an eye on." But Isabelle strung the names into a fabrication of gaiety that would have dazzled a Viennese nobleman. Such is the power of young contralto voices on leather sofas.

I have said that they had reached a very definite stage—nay more—a very critical stage. Kenneth had stayed over a day to meet her and his train left at twelve-eighteen that night. His trunk and suitcase awaited him at the station and his watch was already beginning to worry him and hang heavy in his pocket.

"Isabelle," he said suddenly. "I want to tell you something." They had been talking lightly about "that funny look in her eyes," and on the relative merits of dancing and sitting out, and Isabelle knew from the change in his manner exactly what was coming— indeed she had been wondering how soon it would come. Kenneth reached above their heads and turned out the electric light so that they were in the dark except for the glow from the red lamps that fell through the door from the music room. Then he began:

"I don't know—I don't know whether or not you know what you—what I'm going to say. Lordy Isabelle—this sounds like a line, but it isn't."

"I know," said Isabelle softly.

"I may never see you again—I have darned hard luck sometimes." He was leaning away from her on the other arm of the lounge, but she could see his black eyes plainly in the dark.

"You'll see me again—silly." There was just the slightest emphasis on the last word—so that it became almost a term of endearment. He continued a bit huskily:

"I've fallen for a lot of people—girls—and I guess you have too—boys, I mean but honestly you—" he broke off suddenly and leaned forward, chin on his hands, a favorite and studied gesture. "Oh what's the use, you'll go your way and I suppose I'll go mine."

Silence for a moment. Isabelle was quite stirred—she wound her handkerchief into a tight ball and by the faint light that streamed over her, dropped it deliberately on the floor. Their hands touched for an instant but neither spoke. Silences were becoming more frequent and more delicious. Outside another stray couple had come up and were experimenting on the piano. After the usual preliminary of "chopsticks," one of them started "Babes in the Wood" and a light tenor carried the words into the den—

"Give me your hand
I'll understand
We're off to slumberland."

Isabelle hummed it softly and trembled as she felt Kenneth's hand close over hers.

"Isabelle," he whispered. "You know I'm mad about you. You *do* give a darn about me."

"Yes."

"How much do you care—do you like anyone better?"

"No." He could scarcely hear her, although he bent so near that he felt her breath against his cheek.

"Isabelle, we're going back to school for six long months and why shouldn't we—if I could only just have one thing to remember you by—"

"Close the door." Her voice had just stirred so that he half wondered whether she had spoken at all. As he swung the door softly shut, the music seemed quivering just outside.

"*Moonlight is bright*
Kiss me good-night."

What a wonderful song she thought—everything was wonderful to-night, most of all this romantic scene in the den with their hands clinging and the inevitable looming charmingly close. The future vista of her life seemed an unended succession of scenes like this, under moonlight and pale starlight, and in the backs of warm limousines and in low cosy roadsters stopped under sheltering trees—only the boy might change, and this one was so nice.

"Isabelle!" His whisper blended in the music and they seemed to float nearer together. Her breath came faster. "Can't I kiss you Isabelle—Isabelle?" Lips half parted, she turned her head to him in the dark. Suddenly the ring of voices, the sound of running footsteps surged toward them. Like a flash Kenneth reached up and turned on the light and when the door opened and three boys, the wrathy and dance-craving Peter among them, rushed in, he was turning over the magazines on the table, while she sat, without moving, serene and unembarrassed, and even greeted them with a welcoming smile. But her heart was beating wildly and she felt somehow as if she had been deprived.

It was evidently over. There was a clamour for a dance, there was a glance that passed between them, on his side, despair, on hers, regret, and then the evening went on, with the reassured beaux and the eternal cutting in.

At quarter to twelve Kenneth shook hands with her gravely, in a crowd assembled to wish him good-speed. For an instant he lost his poise and she felt slightly foolish, when a satirical voice from a concealed wit on the edge of the company cried:

"Take her outside, Kenneth." As he took her hand he pressed it a little and she returned the pressure as she had done to twenty hands that evening—that was all.

At two o'clock upstairs Elaine asked her if she and Kenneth had had a "time" in the den. Isabelle turned to her quietly. In her eyes was the light of the idealist, the inviolate dreamer of Joan-like dreams.

"No!" she answered. "I don't do that sort of thing any more—he asked me to, but I said 'No.' "

As she crept into bed she wondered what he'd say in his special delivery to-morrow. He had such a good looking mouth—would she ever—?

"Fourteen angels were watching over them," sang Elaine sleepily from the next room.

"Damn!" muttered Isabelle and punched the pillow into a luxurious lump—"Damn!"

"WINTER DREAMS"

Scott wrote "Winter Dreams" in September 1922 and published it in *Metropolitan* magazine in December. It is the best-known of the stories that he wrote about Ginevra; many of its themes are present in *The Great Gatsby*. The text published here is the magazine version. It includes a passage, on pages 167–68 of the text that follows, which Scott revised and incorporated into *Gatsby* on pages 177–78 of the first edition. The passage (which begins "But what gave it an air of breathless intensity . . .") is a description of Judy Jones's house and an evocation of her former suitors. Fitzgerald cut the passage from "Winter Dreams" when he reprinted it in *All the Sad Young Men*. He made other revisions as well to minimize the similarities between the story and *Gatsby*.

WINTER DREAMS

Some of the caddies were poor as sin and lived in one-room houses with a neurasthenic cow in the front yard, but Dexter Green's father owned the second best grocery store in Dillard—the best one was "The Hub," patronized by the wealthy people from Lake Erminie—and Dexter caddied only for pocket-money.

In the fall when the days became crisp and grey and the long Minnesota winter shut down like the white lid of a box, Dexter's skis moved over the snow that hid the fairways of the golf course. At these times the country gave him a feeling of profound melancholy—it offended him that the links should lie in enforced fallowness, haunted by ragged sparrows for the long season. It was dreary, too, that on the tees where the gay colors fluttered in summer there were now only the desolate sand boxes knee-deep in crusted ice. When he crossed the hills the wind blew cold as misery, and if the sun was out he tramped with his eyes squinted up against the hard dimensionless glare.

In April the winter ceased abruptly. The snow ran down into Lake Erminie scarcely tarrying for the early golfers to brave the season with red and black balls. Without elation, without an interval of moist glory the cold was gone.

Dexter knew that there was something dismal about this northern spring, just as he knew there was something gorgeous about the fall. Fall made him clench his hands and tremble and repeat idiotic sentences to himself and make brisk abrupt gestures of command to imaginary audiences and armies. October filled him with hope which November raised to a sort of ecstatic triumph, and in this mood the fleeting brilliant impressions of the summer at Lake Erminie were ready grist to his mill. He became a golf champion and defeated Mr. T. A. Hedrick in a marvelous match played over a hundred times in the fairways of his imagination, a match each detail of which he changed about untiringly—sometimes winning with almost laughable ease, sometimes coming up magnificently from behind. Again, stepping from a Pierce-Arrow automobile, like Mr. Mortimer Jones, he strolled frigidly into the lounge of the Erminie Golf Club—or perhaps, surrounded by an admiring crowd, he gave an exhibition of fancy diving from the springboard of the Erminie Club raft. . . . Among those most impressed was Mr. Mortimer Jones.

And one day it came to pass that Mr. Jones, himself and not his ghost, came up to Dexter, almost with tears in his eyes and said that Dexter was the —— best caddy in the club and wouldn't he decide not to quit if Mr. Jones made it worth his while, because every other —— caddy in the club lost one ball a hole for him—regularly——

"No, sir," said Dexter, decisively, "I don't want to caddy any more." Then, after a pause, "I'm too old."

"You're—why, you're not more than fourteen. Why did you decide just this morning that you wanted to quit? You promised that next week you'd go over to the state tournament with me."

"I decided I was too old."

Dexter handed in his "A Class" badge, collected what money was due him from the caddy master and caught the train for Dillard.

"The best — — caddy I ever saw," shouted Mr. Mortimer Jones over a drink that afternoon. "Never lost a ball! Willing! Intelligent! Quiet! Honest! Grateful!——"

The little girl who had done this was eleven—beautifully ugly as little girls are apt to be who are destined after a few years to be inexpressibly lovely and bring no end of misery to a great number of men. The spark, however, was perceptible. There was a general ungodliness in the way her lips twisted down at the corners when she smiled and in the—Heaven help us!—in the almost passionate quality of her eyes. Vitality is born early in such women. It was utterly in evidence now, shining through her thin frame in a sort of glow.

She had come eagerly out on to the course at nine o'clock with a white linen nurse and five small new golf clubs in a white canvas bag which the nurse was carrying. When Dexter first saw her she was standing by the caddy house, rather ill-at-ease and trying to conceal the fact by engaging her nurse in an obviously unnatural conversation illumined by startling and irrelevant smiles from herself.

"Well, it's certainly a nice day, Hilda," Dexter heard her say; then she drew down the corners of her mouth, smiled and glanced furtively around, her eyes in transit falling for an instant on Dexter.

Then to the nurse:

"Well, I guess there aren't very many people out here this morning, are there?"

The smile again radiant, blatantly artificial—convincing.

"I don't know what we're supposed to do now," said the nurse, looking nowhere in particular.

"Oh, that's all right"—the smile—"I'll fix it up."

Dexter stood perfectly still, his mouth faintly ajar. He knew that if he moved forward a step his stare would be in her line of vision— if he moved backward he would lose his full view of her face— For a moment he had not realized how young she was. Now he remembered having seen her several times the year before—in bloomers.

Suddenly, involuntarily, he laughed, a short abrupt laugh—then, startled by himself, he turned and began to walk quickly away.

"Boy!"

Dexter stopped.

"Boy——"

Beyond question he was addressed. Not only that, but he was treated to that absurd smile, that preposterous smile—the memory of which at least half a dozen men were to carry to the grave.

"Boy, do you know where the golf teacher is?"

"He's giving a lesson."

"Well, do you know where the caddy-master is?"

"He's not here yet this morning."

"Oh." For a moment this baffled her. She stood alternately on her right and left foot.

"We'd like to get a caddy," said the nurse. "Mrs. Mortimer Jones sent us out to play golf and we don't know how without we get a caddy."

Here she was stopped by an ominous glance from Miss Jones, followed immediately by the smile.

"There aren't any caddies here except me," said Dexter to the nurse, "and I got to stay here in charge until the caddy-master gets here."

"Oh."

Miss Jones and her retinue now withdrew and at a proper distance from Dexter became involved in a heated conversation. The conversation was concluded by Miss Jones taking one of the clubs and hitting it on the ground with violence. For further emphasis she raised it again and was about to bring it down smartly upon the nurse's bosom, when the nurse seized the club and twisted it from her hands.

"You darn *fool!*" cried Miss Jones wildly.

Another argument ensued. Realizing that the elements of the comedy were implied in the scene, Dexter several times began to smile but each time slew the smile before it reached maturity. He could not resist the monstrous conviction that the little girl was justified in beating the nurse.

The situation was resolved by the fortuitous appearance of the caddy-master who was appealed to immediately by the nurse.

"Miss Jones is to have a little caddy and this one says he can't go."

"Mr. McKenna said I was to wait here till you came," said Dexter quickly.

"Well, he's here now." Miss Jones smiled cheerfully at the caddy-master. Then she dropped her bag and set off at a haughty mince toward the first tee.

"Well?" The caddy-master turned to Dexter. "What you standing there like a dummy for? Go pick up the young lady's clubs."

"I don't think I'll go out today," said Dexter.

"You don't——"

"I think I'll quit."

The enormity of his decision frightened him. He was a favorite caddy and the thirty dollars a month he earned through the summer was not to be made elsewhere in Dillard. But he had received a strong emotional shock and his perturbation required a violent and immediate outlet.

It is not so simple as that, either. As so frequently would be the case in the future, Dexter was unconsciously dictated to by his winter dreams.

. . .

Now, of course, the quality and the seasonability of these winter dreams varied, but the stuff of them remained. They persuaded Dexter several years later to pass up a business course at the State University—his father, prospering now, would have paid his way— for the precarious advantage of attending an older and more famous university in the East, where he was bothered by his scanty funds. But do not get the impression, because his winter dreams happened to be concerned at first with musings on the rich, that there was any- thing shoddy in the boy. He wanted not association with glittering things and glittering people—he wanted the glittering things them- selves. Often he reached out for the best without knowing why he wanted it—and sometimes he ran up against the mysterious denials and prohibitions in which life indulges. It is with one of those denials and not with his career as a whole that this story deals.

He made money. It was rather amazing. After college he went to the city from which Lake Erminie draws its wealthy patrons. When he was only twenty-three and had been there not quite two years, there were already people who liked to say, "Now *there's* a boy—" All about him rich men's sons were peddling bonds precariously, or investing patrimonies precariously, or plodding through the two dozen volumes of canned rubbish in the "George Washington Commercial Course," but Dexter borrowed a thousand dollars on his college degree and his steady eyes, and bought a partnership in a *laundry*.

It was a small laundry when he went into it. Dexter made a spe- cialty of learning how the English washed fine woolen golf stock- ings without shrinking them. Inside of a year he was catering to the trade who wore knickerbockers. Men were insisting that their shet- land hose and sweaters go to his laundry just as they had insisted on a caddy who could find golf balls. A little later he was doing their wives' lingerie as well—and running five branches in different parts of the city. Before he was twenty-seven he owned the largest string of laundries in his section of the country. It was then that he sold out and went to New York. But the part of his story that concerns us here goes back to when he was making his first big success.

When he was twenty-three Mr. W. L. Hart, one of the grey-haired men who like to say "Now there's a boy"—gave him a guest card to the Lake Erminie Club for over a week-end. So he signed his name one day on the register, and that afternoon played golf in a foursome with Mr. Hart and Mr. Sandwood and Mr. T. A. Hedrick. He did not consider it necessary to remark that he had once carried Mr. Hart's bag over this same links and that he knew every trap and gully with his eyes shut—but he found himself glancing at the four caddies who trailed them, trying to catch a gleam or gesture that would remind him of himself, that would lessen the gap which lay between his past and his future.

It was a curious day, slashed abruptly with fleeting, familiar impressions. One minute he had the sense of being a trespasser—in the next he was impressed by the tremendous superiority he felt toward Mr. T. A. Hedrick, who was a bore and not even a good golfer any more.

Then, because of a ball Mr. Hart lost near the fifteenth green an enormous thing happened. While they were searching the stiff grasses of the rough there was a clear call of "Fore!" from behind a hill in their rear. And as they all turned abruptly from their search a bright new ball sliced abruptly over the hill and caught Mr. T. A. Hedrick rather neatly in the stomach.

Mr. T. A. Hedrick grunted and cursed.

"By Gad!" cried Mr. Hedrick. "They ought to put some of these crazy women off the course. It's getting to be outrageous."

A head and a voice came up together over the hill:

"Do you mind if we go through?"

"You hit me in the stomach!" thundered Mr. Hedrick.

"Did I?" The girl approached the group of men. "I'm sorry. I yelled 'Fore!' "

Her glance fell casually on each of the men. She nodded to Sandwood and then scanned the fairway for her ball.

"Did I bounce off into the rough?"

It was impossible to determine whether this question was ingenuous or malicious. In a moment, however, she left no doubt, for as her partner came up over the hill she called cheerfully.

"Here I am! I'd have gone on the green except that I hit something."

As she took her stance for a short mashie shot, Dexter looked at her closely. She wore a blue gingham dress, rimmed at throat and shoulders with a white edging that accentuated her tan. The quality of exaggeration, of thinness that had made her passionate eyes and down-turning mouth absurd at eleven was gone now. She was arrestingly beautiful. The color in her cheeks was centered like the color in a picture—it was not a "high" color, but a sort of fluctuating and feverish warmth, so shaded that it seemed at any moment it would recede and disappear. This color and the mobility of her mouth gave a continual impression of flux, of intense life, of passionate vitality—balanced only partially by the sad luxury of her eyes.

She swung her mashie impatiently and without interest, pitching the ball into a sandpit on the other side of the green. With a quick insincere smile and a careless "Thank you!" she went on after it.

"That Judy Jones!" remarked Mr. Hedrick on the next tee, as they waited—some moments—for her to play on ahead. "All she needs is to be turned up and spanked for six months and then to be married off to an old-fashioned cavalry captain."

"Gosh, she's good-looking!" said Mr. Sandwood, who was just over thirty.

"Good-looking!" cried Mr. Hedrick contemptuously. "She always looks as if she wanted to be kissed! Turning those big cow-eyes on every young calf in town!"

It is doubtful if Mr. Hedrick intended a reference to the maternal instinct.

"She'd play pretty good golf if she'd try," said Mr. Sandwood.

"She has no form," said Mr. Hedrick solemnly.

"She has a nice figure," said Mr. Sandwood.

"Better thank the Lord she doesn't drive a swifter ball," said Mr. Hart, winking at Dexter. "Come on. Let's go."

Later in the afternoon the sun went down with a riotous swirl of gold and varying blues and scarlets, and left the dry rustling night of western summer. Dexter watched from the verandah of the Erminie Club, watched the even overlap of the waters in the little wind, silver molasses under the harvest moon. Then the moon held a finger to her lips and the lake became a clear pool, pale and quiet. Dexter put on his bathing suit and swam out to the farthest raft, where he stretched dripping on the wet canvas of the spring board.

There was a fish jumping and a star shining and the lights around the lake were gleaming. Over on a dark peninsula a piano was playing the songs of last summer and of summers before that—songs from "The Pink Lady" and "The Chocolate Soldier" and "Mlle. Modiste"—and because the sound of a piano over a stretch of water had always seemed beautiful to Dexter he lay perfectly quiet and listened.*

The tune the piano was playing at that moment had been gay and new five years before when Dexter was a sophomore at college. They had played it at a prom once and because he could not afford the luxury of proms in those days he had stood outside the gymnasium and listened. The sound of the tune and the splash of the fish jumping precipitated in him a sort of ecstasy and it was with that ecstasy he viewed what happened to him now. The ecstasy was a gorgeous appreciation. It was his sense that, for once, he was magnificently atune to life and that everything about him was radiating a brightness and a glamor he might never know again.

A low pale oblong detached itself suddenly from the darkness of the peninsula, spitting forth the reverberate sound of a racing motorboat. Two white streamers of cleft water rolled themselves out behind it and almost immediately the boat was beside him, drowning out the hot tinkle of the piano in the drone of its spray. Dexter, raising himself on his arms, was aware of a figure standing at the wheel, of two dark eyes regarding him over the lengthening space of water—then the boat had gone by and was sweeping in an immense and purposeless circle of spray round and round in the middle of the lake. With equal eccentricity one of the circles flattened out and headed back toward the raft.

"Who's that?" she called, shutting off her motor. She was so near now that Dexter could see her bathing suit, which consisted apparently of pink rompers. "Oh—you're one of the men I hit in the stomach."

---

* Popular Broadway musicals from 1911, 1909, and 1905.

The nose of the boat bumped the raft. After an inexpert struggle, Dexter managed to twist the line around a two-by-four. Then the raft tilted rakishly as she sprang on.

"Well, kiddo," she said huskily, "do you"—she broke off. She had sat herself upon the spring board, found it damp and jumped up quickly,—"do you want to go surf-board riding?"

He indicated that he would be delighted.

"The name is Judy Jones. Ghastly reputation but enormously popular." She favored him with an absurd smirk—rather, what tried to be a smirk, for, twist her mouth as she might, it was not grotesque, it was merely beautiful. "See that house over on the peninsula?"

"No."

"Well, there's a house there that I live in only you can't see it because it's too dark. And in that house there is a fella waiting for me. When he drove up by the door I drove out by the dock because he has watery eyes and asks me if I have an ideal."

There was a fish jumping and a star shining and the lights around the lake were gleaming. Dexter sat beside Judy Jones and she explained how her boat was driven. Then she was in the water, swimming to the floating surf-board with an exquisite crawl. Watching her was as without effort to the eye as watching a branch waving or a sea-gull flying. Her arms, burned to butternut, moved sinuously among the dull platinum ripples, elbow appearing first, casting the forearm back with a cadence of falling water, then reaching out and down stabbing a path ahead.

They moved out into the lake and, turning, Dexter saw that she was kneeling on the low rear of the now up-tilted surf-board.

"Go faster," she called, "fast as it'll go."

Obediently he jammed the lever forward and the white spray mounted at the bow. When he looked around again the girl was standing up on the rushing board, her arms spread ecstatically, her eyes lifted toward the moon.

"It's awful cold, kiddo," she shouted. "What's your name anyways."

"The name is Dexter Green. Would it amuse you to know how good you look back there?"

"Yes," she shouted, "it would amuse me. Except that I'm too cold. Come to dinner tomorrow night."

He kept thinking how glad he was that he had never caddied for this girl. The damp gingham clinging made her like a statue and turned her intense mobility to immobility at last.

"—At seven o'clock," she shouted. "Judy Jones, Girl, who hit man in stomach. Better write it down,"—and then, "Faster—oh, faster!"

Had he been as calm inwardly as he was in appearance, Dexter would have had time to examine his surroundings in detail. He received, however, an enduring impression that the house was the most elaborate he had ever seen. He had known for a long time that it was the finest on Lake Erminie, with a Pompeiian swimming pool and twelve acres of lawn and garden. But what gave it an air of breathless intensity was the sense that it was inhabited by Judy Jones—that it was as casual a thing to her as the little house in the village had once been to Dexter. There was a feeling of mystery in it, of bedrooms upstairs more beautiful and strange than other bedrooms, of gay and radiant activities taking place through these deep corridors and of romances that were not musty and laid already in lavender, but were fresh and breathing and set forth in rich motor cars and in great dances whose flowers were scarcely withered.

They were more real because he could feel them all about him, pervading the air with the shades and echoes of still vibrant emotion.

And so while he waited for her to appear he peopled the soft deep summer room and the sun porch that opened from it with the men who had already loved Judy Jones. He knew the sort of men they were—the men who when he first went to college had entered from the great prep-schools with graceful clothes and the deep tan of healthy summer, who did nothing or anything with the same debonair ease.

Dexter had seen that, in one sense, he was better than these men. He was newer and stronger. Yet in acknowledging to himself that he wished his children to be like them he was admitting that he was but the rough, strong stuff from which this graceful aristocracy eternally sprang.

When, a year before, the time had come when he could wear good clothes, he had known who were the best tailors in America, and the best tailor in America had made him the suit he wore this evening. He had acquired that particular reserve peculiar to his university, that set it off from other universities. He recognized the value to him of such a mannerism and he had adopted it; he knew that to be careless in dress and manner required more confidence than to be careful. But carelessness was for his children. His mother's name had been Krimslich. She was a Bohemian of the peasant class and she had talked broken English to the end of her days. Her son must keep to the set patterns.

He waited for Judy Jones in her house, and he saw these other young men around him. It excited him that many men had loved her. It increased her value in his eyes.

At a little after seven Judy Jones came downstairs. She wore a blue silk afternoon dress. He was disappointed at first that she had not put on something more elaborate, and this feeling was accentuated when, after a brief greeting, she went to the door of a butler's pantry and pushing it open called: "You can have dinner, Martha." He had rather expected that a butler would announce dinner, that there would be a cocktail perhaps. It even offended him that she should know the maid's name.

Then he put these thoughts behind him as they sat down together on a chintz-covered lounge.

"Father and mother won't be here," she said.

"Ought I to be sorry?"

"They're really quite nice," she confessed, as if it had just occurred to her. "I think my father's the best looking man of his age I've ever seen. And mother looks about thirty."

He remembered the last time he had seen her father, and found he was glad the parents were not to be here tonight. They would wonder who he was. He had been born in Keeble, a Minnesota village fifty miles farther north, and he always gave Keeble as his home instead of Dillard. Country towns were well enough to come from if they weren't inconveniently in sight and used as foot-stools by fashionable lakes.

Before dinner he found the conversation unsatisfactory. The beautiful Judy seemed faintly irritable—as much so as it was possible to be with a comparative stranger. They discussed Lake Erminie and its golf course, the surf-board riding of the night before and the cold she had caught, which made her voice more husky and charming than ever. They talked of his university which she had visited frequently during the past two years, and of the nearby city which supplied Lake Erminie with its patrons and whither Dexter would return next day to his prospering laundries.

During dinner she slipped into a moody depression which gave Dexter a feeling of guilt. Whatever petulance she uttered in her throaty voice worried him. Whatever she smiled at—at him, at a silver fork, at nothing—, it disturbed him that her smile could have no root in mirth, or even in amusement. When the red corners of her lips curved down, it was less a smile than an invitation to a kiss.

Then, after dinner, she led him out on the dark sun porch and deliberately changed the atmosphere.

"Do I seem gloomy?" she demanded.

"No, but I'm afraid I'm boring you," he answered quickly.

"You're not. I like you. But I've just had rather an unpleasant afternoon. There was a—man I cared about. He told me out of a clear sky that he was poor as a church-mouse. He'd never even hinted it before. Does this sound horribly mundane?"

"Perhaps he was afraid to tell you."

"I suppose he was," she answered thoughtfully. "He didn't start right. You see, if I'd thought of him as poor—well, I've been mad about loads of poor men, and fully intended to marry them all. But in this case, I hadn't thought of him that way and my interest in him wasn't strong enough to survive the shock."

"I know. As if a girl calmly informed her fiancé that she was a widow. He might not object to widows, but——"

"Let's start right," she suggested suddenly. "Who are you, anyhow?"

For a moment Dexter hesitated. There were two versions of his life that he could tell. There was Dillard and his caddying and his struggle through college, or——

"I'm nobody," he announced. "My career is largely a matter of futures."

"Are you poor?"

"No," he said frankly. "I'm probably making more money than any man my age in the northwest. I know that's an obnoxious remark, but you advised me to start right."

There was a pause. She smiled, and with a touch of amusement.

"You sound like a man in a play."

"It's your fault. You tempted me into being assertive."

Suddenly she turned her dark eyes directly upon him and the corners of her mouth drooped until her face seemed to open like a flower. He dared scarcely to breathe; he had the sense that she was exerting some force upon him, making him overwhelmingly conscious of the youth and mystery that wealth imprisons and preserves, the freshness of many clothes, of cool rooms and gleaming things, safe and proud above the hot struggles of the poor.

The porch was bright with the bought luxury of starshine. The wicker of the settee squeaked fashionably when he put his arm around her, commanded by her eyes. He kissed her curious and lovely mouth and committed himself to the following of a grail.

It began like that—and continued, with varying shades of intensity, on such a note right up to the dénouement. Dexter surrendered a part of himself to the most direct and unprincipled personality with which he had ever come in contact. Whatever the beautiful Judy Jones desired, she went after with the full pressure of her charm. There was no divergence of method, no jockeying for position or premeditation of effects—there was very little mental quality in any of her affairs. She simply made men conscious to the highest degree of her physical loveliness.

Dexter had no desire to change her. Her deficiencies were knit up with a passionate energy that transcended and justified them.

When, as Judy's head lay against his shoulder that first night, she whispered:

"I don't know what's the matter with me. Last night I thought I was in love with a man and tonight I think I'm in love with you——"

——it seemed to him a beautiful and romantic thing to say. It was the exquisite excitability that for the moment he controlled and owned. But a week later he was compelled to view this same quality in a different light. She took him in her roadster to a picnic supper and after supper she disappeared, likewise in her roadster, with another man. Dexter became enormously upset and was scarcely able to be decently civil to the other people present. When she assured him that she had not kissed the other man he knew she was lying— yet he was glad that she had taken the trouble to lie to him.

He was, as he found before the summer ended, one of a dozen, a varying dozen, who circulated about her. Each of them had at one time been favored above all others—about half of them still basked in the solace of occasional sentimental revivals. Whenever one showed signs of dropping out through long neglect she granted him a brief honeyed hour which encouraged him to tag along for a year or so longer. Judy made these forays upon the helpless and defeated without malice, indeed half unconscious that there was anything mischievous in what she did.

When a new man came to town everyone dropped out—dates were automatically cancelled.

The helpless part of trying to do anything about it was that she did it all herself. She was not a girl who could be "won" in the kinetic sense—she was proof against cleverness, she was proof against charm. If any of these assailed her too strongly she would immediately resolve the affair to a physical basis and under the magic of her physical splendor the strong as well as the brilliant played her game and not their own. She was entertained only by the gratification of her desires and by the direct exercise of her own charm. Perhaps from so much youthful love, so many youthful lovers, she had come, in self defense, to nourish herself wholly from within.

Succeeding Dexter's first exhilaration came restlessness and dissatisfaction. The helpless ecstasy of losing himself in her charm was a powerful opiate rather than a tonic. It was fortunate for his work during the winter that those moments of ecstasy came infrequently. Early in their acquaintance it had seemed for a while that there was a deep and spontaneous mutual attraction—that first August for example—three days of long evenings on her dusky verandah, of strange wan kisses through the late afternoon, in shadowy alcoves or behind the protecting trellises of the garden arbors, of mornings when she was fresh as a dream and almost shy at meeting him in the clarity of the rising day. There was all the ecstasy of an engagement about it, sharpened by his realization that there was no engagement. It was during those three days that, for the first time, he had asked her to marry him. She said "maybe some day," she said "kiss me," she said "I'd like to marry you," she said "I love you,"—she said— nothing.

The three days were interrupted by the arrival of a New York man who visited the Jones' for half September. To Dexter's agony, rumor engaged them. The man was the son of the president of a great trust company. But at the end of a month it was reported that Judy was yawning. At a dance one night she sat all evening in a motor boat with an old beau, while the New Yorker searched the club for her frantically. She told the old beau that she was bored with her visitor and two days later he left. She was seen with him at the station and it was reported that he looked very mournful indeed.

. . .

On this note the summer ended. Dexter was twenty-four and he found himself increasingly in a position to do as he wished. He joined two clubs in the city and lived at one of them. Though he was by no means an integral part of the stag-lines at these clubs he managed to be on hand at dances where Judy Jones was likely to appear. He could have gone out socially as much as he liked—he was an eligible young man, now, and popular with downtown fathers. His confessed devotion to Judy Jones had rather solidified his position. But he had no social aspirations and rather despised the dancing men who were always on tap for the Thursday or Saturday parties and who filled in at dinners with the younger married set. Already he was playing with the idea of going east to New York. He wanted to take Judy Jones with him. No disillusion as to the world in which she had grown up could cure his illusion as to her desirability.

Remember that—for only in the light of it can what he did for her be understood.

Eighteen months after he first met Judy Jones he became engaged to another girl. Her name was Irene Scheerer and her father was one of the men who had always believed in Dexter. Irene was light haired and sweet and honorable and a little stout and she had two beaus whom she pleasantly relinquished when Dexter formally asked her to marry him.

Summer, fall, winter, spring, another summer, another fall—so much he had given of his active life to the curved lips of Judy Jones. She had treated him with interest, with encouragement, with malice, with indifference, with contempt. She had inflicted on him the innumerable little slights and indignities possible in such a case—as if in revenge for having ever cared for him at all. She had beckoned him and yawned at him and beckoned him again and he had responded often with bitterness and narrowed eyes. She had brought him ecstatic happiness and intolerable agony of spirit. She had caused him untold inconvenience and not a little trouble. She had insulted him and she had ridden over him and she had played his interest in her against his interest in his work—for fun. She had done everything to him except to criticise him—this she had not done—it seemed to him only because it might have sullied the utter indifference she manifested and sincerely felt toward him.

When autumn had come and gone again it occurred to him that he could not have Judy Jones. He had to beat this into his mind but he convinced himself at last. He lay awake at night for a while and argued it over. He told himself the trouble and the pain she had caused him, he enumerated her glaring deficiencies as a wife. Then he said to himself that he loved her and after a while he fell asleep. For a week, lest he imagine her husky voice over the telephone or her eyes opposite him at lunch, he worked hard and late, and at night he went to his office and plotted out his years.

At the end of a week he went to a dance and cut in on her once. For almost the first time since they had met he did not ask her to sit out with him or tell her that she was lovely. It hurt him that she did not miss these things—that was all. He was not jealous when he saw that there was a new man tonight. He had been hardened against jealousy long before.

He stayed late at the dance. He sat for an hour with Irene Scheerer and talked about books and about music. He knew very little about either. But he was beginning to be master of his own time now and he had a rather priggish notion that he—the young and already fabulously successful Dexter Green—should know more about such things.

That was in October when he was twenty-five. In January Dexter and Irene became engaged. It was to be announced in June and they were to be married three months later.

The Minnesota winter prolonged itself interminably and it was almost May when the winds came soft and the snow ran down into Lake Erminie at last. For the first time in over a year Dexter was enjoying a certain tranquility of spirit. Judy Jones had been in Florida and afterwards in Hot Springs and somewhere she had been engaged and somewhere she had broken it off. At first, when Dexter had definitely given her up, it had made him sad that people still linked them together and asked for news of her, but when he began to be placed at dinner next to Irene Scheerer people didn't ask him about her any more—they told him about her. He ceased to be an authority on her.

May at last. Dexter walked the streets at night when the darkness was damp as rain, wondering that so soon, with so little done, so much of ecstasy had gone from him. May, one year back had been marked by Judy's poignant, unforgivable, yet forgiven turbulence—it had been one of those rare times when he fancied she had grown to care for him. That old penny's worth of happiness he had spent for this bushel of content. He knew that Irene would be no more than a curtain spread behind him, a hand moving among gleaming tea cups, a voice calling to children . . . fire and loveliness were gone, magic of night and the hushed wonder of the hours and seasons . . . slender lips, down-turning, dropping to his lips like poppy petals, bearing him up into a heaven of eyes . . . a haunting gesture, light of a warm lamp on her hair. The thing was deep in him. He was too strong, too alive for it to die lightly.

In the middle of May when the weather balanced for a few days on the thin bridge that led to deep summer he turned in one night at Irene's house. Their engagement was to be announced in a week now—no one would be surprised at it. And tonight they would sit together on the lounge at the College Club and look on for an hour at the dancers. It gave him a sense of solidity to go with her—— She was so sturdily popular, so intensely a "good egg."

He mounted the steps of the brown stone house and stepped inside.

"Irene," he called.

Mrs. Scheerer came out of the living room to meet him.

"Dexter," she said, "Irene's gone upstairs with a splitting headache. She wanted to go with you but I made her go to bed."

"Nothing serious I——"

"Oh, no. She's going to play golf with you in the morning. You can spare her for just one night, can't you, Dexter?"

Her smile was kind. She and Dexter liked each other. In the living room he talked for a moment before he said goodnight.

Returning to the College Club, where he had rooms, he stood in the doorway for a moment and watched the dancers. He leaned against the door post, nodded at a man or two—yawned.

"Hello, kiddo."

The familiar voice at his elbow startled him. Judy Jones had left a man and crossed the room to him—Judy Jones, a slender enamelled doll in cloth of gold, gold in a band at her head, gold in two slipper points at her dress's hem. The fragile glow of her face seemed to blossom as she smiled at him. A breeze of warmth and light blew through the room. His hands in the pockets of his dinner jacket tightened spasmodically. He was filled with a sudden excitement.

"When did you get back?" he asked casually.

"Come here and I'll tell you about it."

She turned and he followed her. She had been away—he could have wept at the wonder of her return. She had passed through enchanted streets, doing young things that were like plaintive music. All mysterious happenings, all fresh and quickening hopes, had gone away with her, come back with her now.

She turned in the doorway.

"Have you a car here? If you haven't I have."

"I have a coupé."

In, then, with a rustle of golden cloth. He slammed the door. Into so many cars she had stepped—like this—like that—her back against the leather, so—her elbow resting on the door—waiting. She would have been soiled long since had there been anything to soil her,—except herself—but these things were all her own outpouring.

With an effort he forced himself to start the car and avoiding her surprised glance backed into the street. This was nothing, he must remember. She had done this before and he had put her behind him, as he would have slashed a bad account from his books.

He drove slowly downtown and affecting a disinterested abstraction traversed the deserted streets of the business section, peopled here and there, where a movie was giving out its crowd or where consumptive or pugilistic youth lounged in front of pool halls. The clink of glasses and the slap of hands on the bars issued from saloons, cloisters of glazed glass and dirty yellow light.

She was watching him closely and the silence was embarrassing yet in this crisis he could find no casual word with which to profane the hour. At a convenient turning he began to zig-zag back toward the College Club.

"Have you missed me?" she asked suddenly.

"Everybody missed you."

He wondered if she knew of Irene Scheerer. She had been back only a day—her absence had been almost contemporaneous with his engagement.

"What a remark!" Judy laughed sadly—without sadness. She looked at him searchingly. He became absorbed for a moment in the dashboard.

"You're handsomer than you used to be," she said thoughtfully. "Dexter, you have the most rememberable eyes."

He could have laughed at this, but he did not laugh. It was the sort of thing that was said to sophomores. Yet it stabbed at him.

"I'm awfully tired of everything, kiddo." She called everyone kiddo, endowing the obsolete slang with careless, individual camaraderie. "I wish you'd marry me."

The directness of this confused him. He should have told her now that he was going to marry another girl but he could not tell her. He could as easily have sworn that he had never loved her.

"I think we'd get along," she continued, on the same note, "unless probably you've forgotten me and fallen in love with another girl."

Her confidence was obviously enormous. She had said, in effect, that she found such a thing impossible to believe, that if it were true he had merely committed a childish indiscretion—and probably to show off. She would forgive him, because it was not a matter of any moment but rather something to be brushed aside lightly.

"Of course you could never love anybody but me," she continued. "I like the way you love me. Oh, Dexter, have you forgotten last year?"

"No, I haven't forgotten."

"Neither have I!"

Was she sincerely moved—or was she carried along by the wave of her own acting?

"I wish we could be like that again," she said, and he forced himself to answer:

"I don't think we can."

"I suppose not. . . . I hear you're giving Irene Scheerer a violent rush."

There was not the faintest emphasis on the name, yet Dexter was suddenly ashamed.

"Oh, take me home," cried Judy suddenly, "I don't want to go back to that idiotic dance—with those children."

Then, as he turned up the street that led to the residence district, Judy began to cry quietly to herself. He had never seen her cry before.

The dark street lightened, the dwellings of the rich loomed up around them, he stopped his coupé in front of the great white bulk of the Mortimer Jones' house, somnolent, gorgeous, drenched with the splendor of the damp moonlight. Its solidity startled him. The strong walls, the fine steel of the girders, the breadth and beam and pomp of it were there only to bring out the contrast with the young beauty beside him. It was sturdy to accentuate her slightness—as if to show what a breeze could be generated by a butterfly's wing.

He sat perfectly quiet, his nerves in wild clamor, afraid that if he moved he would find her irresistibly in his arms. Two tears had rolled down her wet face and trembled on her upper lip.

"I'm more beautiful than anybody else," she said brokenly. "Why can't I be happy?" Her moist eyes tore at his stability—mouth turned slowly downward with an exquisite sadness. "I'd like to marry you if you'll have me, Dexter. I suppose you think I'm not worth having but I'll be so beautiful for you, Dexter."

A million phrases of anger, of pride, of passion, of hatred, of tenderness fought on his lips. Then a perfect wave of emotion washed over him, carrying off with it a sediment of wisdom, of convention, of doubt, of honor. This was his girl who was speaking, his own, his beautiful, his pride.

"Won't you come in?" he heard her draw in her breath sharply.

Waiting.

"All right," his voice was trembling, "I'll come in."

It seems strange to say that neither when it was over nor a long time afterward did he regret that night. Looking at it from the perspective of ten years, the fact that Judy's flare for him endured just one month seemed of little importance. Nor did it matter that by his yielding he subjected himself to a deeper agony in the end and gave serious hurt to Irene Scheerer and to Irene's parents who had befriended him. There was nothing sufficiently pictorial about Irene's grief to stamp itself on his mind.

Dexter was at bottom hard-minded. The attitude of the city on his action was of no importance to him, not because he was going to leave the city, but because any outside attitude on the situation seemed superficial. He was completely indifferent to popular opinion. Nor, when he had seen that it was no use, that he did not possess in himself the power to move fundamentally or to hold Judy Jones, did he bear any malice toward her. He loved her and he would love her until the day he was too old for loving—but he could not have her. So he tasted the deep pain that is reserved only for the strong, just as he had tasted for a little while the deep happiness.

Even the ultimate falsity of the grounds upon which Judy terminated the engagement—that she did not want to "take him away" from Irene, that it was on her conscience—did not revolt him. He was beyond any revulsion or any amusement.

He went east in February with the intention of selling out his laundries and settling in New York—but the war came to America in March and changed his plans. He returned to the West, handed over the management of the business to his partner and went into the first officers' training camp in late April. He was one of those young thousands who greeted the war with a certain amount of relief, welcoming the liberation from webs of tangled emotion.

This story is not his biography, remember, although things creep into it which have nothing to do with those dreams he had when he was young. We are almost done with them and with him now. There is only one more incident to be related here and it happens seven years farther on.

It took place in New York, where he had done well—so well that there were no barriers too high for him now. He was thirty-two years old, and, except for one flying trip immediately after the war, he had not been west in seven years. A man named Devlin from Detroit came into his office to see him in a business way, and then and there this incident occurred, and closed out, so to speak, this particular side of his life.

"So you're from the Middle West," said the man Devlin with careless curiosity. "That's funny—I thought men like you were probably born and raised on Wall Street. You know—wife of one of my best friends in Detroit came from your city. I was an usher at the wedding."

Dexter waited with no apprehension of what was coming. There was a magic that his city would never lose for him. Just as Judy's house had always seemed to him more mysterious and gay than other houses, so his dream of the city itself, now that he had gone from it, was pervaded with a melancholy beauty.

"Judy Simms," said Devlin with no particular interest. "Judy Jones she was once."

"Yes, I knew her." A dull impatience spread over him. He had heard, of course, that she was married,—perhaps deliberately he had heard no more.

"Awfully nice girl," brooded Devlin, meaninglessly. "I'm sort of sorry for her."

"Why?" Something in Dexter was alert, receptive, at once.

"Oh, Joe Simms has gone to pieces in a way. I don't mean he beats her, you understand, or anything like that. But he drinks and runs around——"

"Doesn't she run around?"

"No. Stays at home with her kids."

"Oh."

"She's a little too old for him," said Devlin.

"Too old!" cried Dexter. "Why man, she's only twenty-seven."

He was possessed with a wild notion of rushing out into the streets and taking a train to Detroit. He rose to his feet, spasmodically, involuntarily.

"I guess you're busy," Devlin apologized quickly. "I didn't realize——"

"No, I'm not busy," said Dexter, steadying his voice, "I'm not busy at all. Not busy at all. Did you say she was—twenty-seven. No, I said she was twenty-seven."

"Yes, you did," agreed Devlin drily.

"Go on, then. Go on."

"What do you mean?"

"About Judy Jones."

Devlin looked at him helplessly.

"Well, that's—I told you all there is to it. He treats her like the devil. Oh, they're not going to get divorced or anything. When he's particularly outrageous she forgives him. In fact, I'm inclined to think she loves him. She was a pretty girl when she first came to Detroit."

A pretty girl! The phrase struck Dexter as ludicrous.

"Isn't she—a pretty girl any more?"

"Oh, she's all right."

"Look here," said Dexter, sitting down suddenly. "I don't understand. You say she was a 'pretty girl' and now you say she's 'all right.' I don't understand what you mean—Judy Jones wasn't a pretty girl, at all. She was a great beauty. Why, I knew her, I knew her. She was——"

Devlin laughed pleasantly.

"I'm not trying to start a row," he said. "I think Judy's a nice girl and I like her. I can't understand how a man like Joe Simms could fall madly in love with her, but he did." Then he added, "Most of the women like her."

Dexter looked closely at Devlin, thinking wildly that there must be a reason for this, some insensitivity in the man or some private malice.

"Lots of women fade just-like-*that*," Devlin snapped his fingers. "You must have seen it happen. Perhaps I've forgotten how pretty she was at her wedding. I've seen her so much since then, you see. She has nice eyes."

A sort of dullness settled down upon Dexter. For the first time in his life he felt like getting very drunk. He knew that he was laughing loudly at something Devlin had said but he did not know what it was or why it was funny. When Devlin went, in a few minutes, he lay down on his lounge and looked out the window at the New York skyline into which the sun was sinking in dull lovely shades of pink and gold.

He had thought that having nothing else to lose he was invulnerable at last—but he knew that he had just lost something more, as surely as if he had married Judy Jones and seen her fade away before his eyes.

The dream was gone. Something had been taken from him. In a sort of panic he pushed the palms of his hands into his eyes and tried to bring up a picture of the waters lapping at Lake Erminie and the moonlit verandah, and gingham on the golf links and the dry sun and the gold color of her neck's soft down. And her mouth damp to his kisses and her eyes plaintive with melancholy and her freshness like new fine linen in the morning. Why, these things were no longer in the world. They had existed and they existed no more.

For the first time in years the tears were streaming down his face. But they were for himself now. He did not care about mouth and eyes and moving hands. He wanted to care and he could not care. For he had gone away and he could never go back any more. The gates were closed, the sun was gone down and there was no beauty but the grey beauty of steel that withstands all time. Even the grief he could have borne was left behind in the country of illusion, of youth, of the richness of life, where his winter dreams had flourished.

"Long ago," he said, "long ago, there was something in me, but now that thing is gone. Now that thing is gone, that thing is gone. I cannot cry. I cannot care. That thing will come back no more."

OTHER GINEVRAS

Leonardo's portrait of Ginevra de Benci. National Gallery of Art.

Leonardo da Vinci's portrait of Ginevra de Benci, the source of Ginevra King's name, is one of his most celebrated paintings. Ginevra de Benci, born in 1457, was the daughter of a prosperous

Florentine banker who was closely allied with the Medici family. In 1474, at the age of sixteen, Ginevra was matched in an arranged marriage with Luigi Niccolini, a wealthy widower sixteen years her senior. Leonardo's portrait of Ginevra, painted in the year of her wedding, captures a melancholy expression; she is said to have been unhappy in the marriage. The painting, more than a simple likeness, is believed to be among the first portraits in western art to capture mood, emotion, and character in its human subject.

In the late 1470s, Ginevra de Benci was adopted as an object of platonic devotion (after the local fashion) by Bernardo Bembo, a Venetian ambassador to the court of Lorenzo the Magnificent. Bembo wrote poems to Ginevra in the Petrarchan manner, as did Cristoforo Landino and Alessandro Braccesi, two poets in the Medici circle. Lorenzo himself addressed two sonnets to Ginevra, praising her beauty and virtue.

Ginevra de Benci died in 1520. From that date until 1741 the location of Leonardo's portrait of her is unknown. During the years 1741–1967, the painting was part of the Liechtenstein Collection; in 1944, it was hidden in a monastery to prevent its falling into the hands of Russian troops. The National Gallery of Art in Washington, D.C., acquired the portrait in 1967 for five million dollars. It was restored in 1991 and hangs today in Gallery 6 on the West Main Floor of that institution.

In Italian folklore one finds another tale about a young bride named Ginevra. This Ginevra plays hide-and-seek on her wedding day; in an old and abandoned part of a castle she secrets herself in a large trunk, but the lid falls and she is trapped by a spring lock. She cannot be found. Years later the trunk is sold, and her skeleton is discovered. This tale is the basis for C. A. Somerset's two-act drama *The Mistletoe Bough, or, Young Lovel's Bride* (1834) and for the ballad "The Mistletoe Bough" (1884) by Thomas Haynes Bayley. The final stanza of Bayley's poem reads this way:

How sad the day when in sportive jest
She hid from her lord in the old oak chest,
It closed with a spring and a dreadful doom,
And the bride lay clasped in a living tomb.
Oh, the mistletoe bough,
Oh, the mistletoe bough.

The American author James Lane Allen wrote a novel-length version of the "Ginevra" story that he called *The Bride of the Mistletoe* (1909). Ginevra King mentions the book in a March 25, 1915, letter to Scott, included in Appendix 2 of this book. In that same letter she tells him: "Shelly or Keats wrote a horrible one about a Ginevra too. They always seem to have something perfectly dreadful happen to them on their wedding day." Ginevra has in mind Shelley's unfinished poem "Ginevra," composed in Pisa in 1821 and published by Mary Shelley in 1824, after the poet's death. Fitzgerald likely knew the poem; he steeped himself in Shelley's verse during his Princeton years and was able to quote long passages from memory throughout his adult life.

Shelley based his "Ginevra" on two sources, one literary and one from his own life. Both involved arranged marriages. The literary source is a story found in Marco Lastri's *L'Osservatore Fiorentino,* a guide to Italian antiquities; Mary Shelley copied out the narrative and showed it to her husband in 1821. In this tale, set in the 1490s, a Florentine maiden named Ginevra degli Almieri is wed, against her will, to Francesco Agolanti. She is in love with Antonio Rondinelli but is compelled by her father to enter the arranged marriage. After the wedding her health declines, and she enters a swoon so deep that she is thought to have died. Her body is placed in the family vault. Ginevra awakens and goes to her husband's house, then to her father's, but both men believe her to be a ghost and refuse her entry. She flees to Antonio, who takes her in and restores her to health; eventually the church dissolves her marriage to Francesco, and she and Antonio are free to wed.

This tale became merged in Shelley's mind with the real-life story of Teresa Viviani, a beautiful and intelligent young woman whom the Shelleys met in November 1820 and came to call by the name Emilia. This woman had been shut away in a convent by her parents at the age of sixteen; her only possible escape was through an arranged marriage. Shelley became strongly attached to Emilia and, with his wife, helped to guide her into a marriage with a wealthy older man, Luigi Biondi, in September 1821. The marriage did not last; Emilia left her husband in 1826, four years after Shelley's death.

Shelley's poem, in heroic couplets, is filled with imagery that would have appealed to Fitzgerald, as would the twin elements of arranged marriage and the authority of money. Herewith lines 13–27 from Shelley's "Ginevra":

And so she moved under the bridal veil,
Which made the paleness of her cheek more pale,
And deepened the faint crimson of her mouth,
And darkened her dark locks, as moonlight doth,—
And of the gold and jewels glittering there
She scarce felt conscious, but the weary glare
Lay like a chaos of unwelcome light,
Vexing the sense with gorgeous undelight.

A moonbeam in the shadow of a cloud
Was less heavenly fair—her face was bowed,
And as she passed, the diamonds in her hair
Were mirrored in the polished marble stair
Which led from the cathedral to the street;
And even as she went her light fair feet
Erased these images.

NOTES

PAGE xiv: GINEVRA CORRESPONDED . . . The letters between
Ginevra King Pirie and Arthur Mizener are among Mizener's papers
at Princeton University Library.

PAGE xiv: MOST OF FITZGERALD'S BIOGRAPHERS . . . In-
sightful remarks about Ginevra's role in Fitzgerald's life are found
in Mizener's *The Far Side of Paradise* (Boston: Houghton Mifflin,
1951; rev. ed. 1965) and in Scott Donaldson's *Fool for Love: F. Scott
Fitzgerald* (New York: Congdon and Weed, 1983). Mizener quotes
from Ginevra's letters to him; Donaldson is especially perceptive
about Fitzgerald's relationship with Ginevra. Other biographies are
Andrew Turnbull, *Scott Fitzgerald* (New York: Scribners, 1962);
Henry Dan Piper, *F. Scott Fitzgerald: A Critical Portrait* (New York:
Holt Rinehart and Winston, 1965); Matthew J. Bruccoli, *Some Sort
of Epic Grandeur: The Life of F. Scott Fitzgerald* (New York: Har-
court Brace Jovanovich, 1981); André Le Vot, *F. Scott Fitzgerald: A
Biography* (Garden City, N.Y.: Doubleday, 1983); Jeffrey Meyers,
Scott Fitzgerald (New York: HarperCollins, 1994); Kendall Taylor,
*Sometimes Madness Is Wisdom: Zelda and Scott Fitzgerald, a Mar-
riage* (New York: Ballantine, 2001). See also a recent biography of

Zelda by Sally Cline, *Zelda Fitzgerald: Her Voice in Paradise* (New York: Arcade Publ., 2002). In her seminal biography, *Zelda* (New York: Harper and Row, 1970), Nancy Milford does not comment on Ginevra.

Arthur Mizener had access to the transcripts of Ginevra's letters to Scott but saw them only toward the end of his work on *The Far Side of Paradise*. He was able to work only one quotation into his text—a sentence from Ginevra's July 7, 1917, letter to Scott telling him that she had destroyed his letters (rev. ed., p. 61). The quotation is typed on an index card; the card is paper-clipped to the final typescript of the biography, preserved among Mizener's papers at Princeton. Turnbull also saw the transcripts and, on p. 56 of *Scott Fitzgerald*, quoted one sentence from them—a sentence that Ginevra had copied from one of Scott's letters. Neither Mizener nor Turnbull mentions the story that Ginevra wrote for Scott in May 1916. It's possible that neither man read that far into the transcripts. Mizener and Turnbull are the only biographers to have seen the letters; other Fitzgerald biographers have used Mizener's or Turnbull's quotes. So far as I can determine, no biographer has ever seen the diary.

PAGE 10: MISS HILLARD HAD TAUGHT . . . Archibald MacLeish was one of Mary Hillard's nephews. She played an important role in his life, introducing him to his future wife (a Westover girl) and attempting to discourage him from becoming a poet. For details, see Scott Donaldson, *Archibald MacLeish: An American Life* (Boston: Houghton Mifflin, 1992), esp. pp. 46–47, 68–69, and 118–21.

PAGE 15: "IF IT WEREN'T . . . Mizener, *The Far Side of Paradise*, rev. ed., p. 16.

PAGE 18: "SCOTT WAS ON . . . Norris Jackson, quoted in Lloyd C. Hackl, "*Still Home to Me*": *F. Scott Fitzgerald and St. Paul, Minnesota* (St. Paul: privately published, 1996): 44.

PAGE 24: "PARDON ME . . . Quoted in Turnbull, *Scott Fitzgerald:* 55. Fitzgerald pasted the handwritten draft of the wire into his scrapbook; it is facsimiled on p. 26 of this book.

PAGE 35: REUBEN WARNER . . . DEERING DAVIS . . . Reuben had written Scott a letter in which he claimed to have held hands with Ginevra during an automobile ride after Scott had left St. Paul. See Turnbull, *Scott Fitzgerald:* 55–56. Deering Davis, the son and grandson of prominent Chicago physicians, married the Hollywood actress Louise Brooks in October 1933; the marriage ended in divorce the following March.

PAGE 40: "MADE LUMINOUS . . . "My Lost City," *The Crack-Up*, ed. Edmund Wilson (New York: New Directions, 1945): 24.

PAGE 46: "THREE HUNDRED YOUNG LADIES . . . *Daily Princetonian*, January 7, 1916; quoted in Mizener, *The Far Side of Paradise*, rev. ed., p. 61n.

PAGE 57: "A CATHOLIC ELEMENT . . . Fitzgerald to Perkins, June 20, 1922, in *Dear Scott/Dear Max: The Fitzgerald–Perkins Correspondence*, ed. John Kuehl and Jackson R. Bryer (New York: Scribners, 1971): 61.

PAGE 59: (FITZGERALD IDENTIFIED . . . Fitzgerald to Perkins, December 20, 1924, *Dear Scott/ Dear Max:* 90.

PAGE 61: "POOR BOYS . . . Fitzgerald recorded the words within quotation marks, but without attribution, in his personal ledger under the entry for August 1916. *F. Scott Fitzgerald's Ledger: A Facsimile,* ed. Matthew J. Bruccoli (Washington, D.C.: Microcard, 1972): 170. The entry is facsimiled on p. 62 of this book.

PAGE 62: "MY GIRLFRIEND . . . Elizabeth Friskey, "Visiting the Golden Girl," *Princeton Alumni Weekly,* October 8, 1974: 11.

PAGE 69: HE PROBABLY DID NOT ATTEND . . . It would have been difficult for Fitzgerald, who was stationed in Montgomery, to have secured enough leave time to attend Ginevra's wedding in Chicago. It's possible that he managed the journey: toward the end of his life, on one of the endpapers of his copy of Malraux's *Man's Hope* (1938), he made some notes about his sources for *The Great Gatsby.* Note IV-B reads: "Memory of Ginevra's Wedding." I know of no other indication, either in Fitzgerald's letters or his notebooks, that he was present at the ceremony. The endpaper is facsimiled in the introduction to *The Great Gatsby,* ed. Matthew J. Bruccoli (Cambridge and New York: Cambridge University Press, 1991): xiv.

PAGE 82: IN THE SPOTLIGHT . . . For headlines and quotes about the robbery, see the front-page accounts in the *Chicago Tribune,* November 22 and 23, 1931.

PAGE 85: HOW MUCH OF HIS WORK SHE READ . . . In a letter to Mizener of May 12, 1948, Ginevra says that she has read *This Side of Paradise, The Beautiful and Damned, The Great Gatsby,* and *The Crack-Up.* At Mizener's suggestion she read the three Josephine stories included in *Taps at Reveille.*

PAGE 85: HE CONTACTED HER . . . Perhaps understandably, because he was still married to Zelda, Fitzgerald told his daughter, Scottie, that Ginevra had contacted *him* and suggested that they meet. For the letter, dated October 8, 1937, see *The Letters of F. Scott Fitzgerald*, ed. Andrew Turnbull (New York: Scribners, 1963): 19. In a letter to Mizener dated May 12, 1948, Ginevra writes that Fitzgerald got in touch with her first, and that she was nervous about seeing him.

PAGE 86: SHE WAS THE FIRST GIRL . . . Fitzgerald to Scottie Fitzgerald, October 8, 1936, *Letters*, ed. Turnbull: 19.

PAGE 87: ON THIS NOTE . . . The account of the luncheon is taken from Ginevra to Mizener, May 12, 1948. Fitzgerald's comment (which Ginevra related to her daughter and granddaughter in conversation) is quoted in Dinitia Smith, "Love Notes Drenched in Moonlight," *New York Times*, September 8, 2003: B5.

PAGE 91: FITZGERALD COPIED NOTHING . . . He might have taken the title of his last Triangle show, *Safety First!* (1916–17), from a letter that Ginevra wrote to him on February 19, 1916. In that letter, she described a club that she and five other Westover girls had formed. It was called "The Bunch," or "K.I.D.S." (for "Keep It Dark"). Their pledge pins were simple safety pins, and their motto was "Safety First!"

Ginevra wrote as follows to Scott on March 5, 1915: "Just wrote a classy theme on going home on the train and when I had finished it, I honestly thought I was getting off the train at Chicago." One thinks immediately of the famous passage in *The Great Gatsby* (pp. 211–12 of the first edition) in which Fitzgerald describes the train rides that midwestern teenagers who were prepping in the East took home for Christmas vacation. Ginevra does not mention her theme again in this letter or in any later letter to Scott. An early version of the passage in *Gatsby* occurs in the surviving drafts of *The Romantic Egotist*, the predecessor to *This Side of Paradise*. This passage, which dates from 1917–18, is quoted in James L. W. West III, *The Making of "This Side of Paradise"* (Philadelphia: University of Pennsylvania Press, 1983): 32.

PAGE 91: "MY FIRST GIRL . . . in *These Stories Went to Market*, ed. Vernon McKenzie (New York: McBride, 1935): xviii.

PAGE 94: MOSTLY, WE AUTHORS . . . "One Hundred False Starts," *Afternoon of an Author*, ed. Arthur Mizener (Princeton, N.J.: Princeton University Press, 1957): 132. The essay first appeared in the *Saturday Evening Post*, March 4, 1933.

SELECTED BIBLIOGRAPHY

Anon. *The History of Onwentsia, 1895–1945.* Lake Forest, Ill.: Onwentsia Club, 1984.

Bruccoli, Matthew J., ed. *F. Scott Fitzgerald's Ledger: A Facsimile.* Washington, D.C.: Microcard, 1972.

———. *Some Sort of Epic Grandeur: The Life of F. Scott Fitzgerald.* New York: Harcourt Brace Jovanovich, 1981.

Bruccoli, Matthew J., and Margaret M. Duggan, eds. *Correspondence of F. Scott Fitzgerald.* New York: Random House, 1980.

Coventry, Kim, Daniel Meyer, and Arthur H. Miller. *Classic Country Estates of Lake Forest: Architecture and Landscape Design 1856–1940.* New York: Norton, 2003.

Donaldson, Scott. *Fool for Love: F. Scott Fitzgerald.* New York: Congdon and Weed, 1983.

Friskey, Elizabeth. "Visiting the Golden Girl." *Princeton Alumni Weekly,* October 8, 1974: 10–11.

Ginevra's Story: Solving the Mysteries of Leonardo da Vinci's First Known Portrait. National Gallery of Art. Home Vision Arts, 1999. Videocassette.

Hook, Andrew. *F. Scott Fitzgerald: A Literary Life.* Basingstoke, Hampshire: Palgrave, 2002.

Kuehl, John, ed. *The Apprentice Fiction of F. Scott Fitzgerald: 1909–1917.* New Brunswick, N.J.: Rutgers University Press, 1965.

Kuehl, John, and Jackson R. Bryer, eds. *Dear Scott/Dear Max: The Fitzgerald–Perkins Correspondence.* New York: Scribners, 1971.

Le Vot, André. *F. Scott Fitzgerald: A Biography.* Transl. William Byron. Garden City, N.Y.: Doubleday, 1983.

Mangum, Bryant. *A Fortune Yet: Money in the Art of F. Scott Fitzgerald's Short Stories.* New York: Garland, 1991.

Marsden, Donald. *The Long Kickline: A History of the Princeton Triangle Club.* Princeton, N.J.: Triangle Club, 1968.

Meyers, Jeffrey. *Scott Fitzgerald: A Biography.* New York: Harper-Collins, 1994.

Milford, Nancy. *Zelda: A Biography.* New York: Harper and Row, 1970.

Mizener, Arthur. *The Far Side of Paradise: A Biography of F. Scott Fitzgerald.* Boston: Houghton Mifflin, 1951. Rev. ed., 1965.

Noden, Merrell. "Fitzgerald's First Love." *Princeton Alumni Weekly,* November 5, 2003: 19–21.

Piper, Henry Dan. *F. Scott Fitzgerald: A Critical Portrait.* New York: Holt, Rinehart and Winston, 1965.

Smith, Dinitia. "Love Notes Drenched in Moonlight." *New York Times,* Sept. 8, 2003. Arts Section: B1ff.

Spykman, Elizabeth Choate. *Westover: 1909–1959.* Middlebury, Conn.: Westover School, 1959.

Taylor, Kendall. *Sometimes Madness Is Wisdom: Zelda and Scott Fitzgerald, a Marriage.* New York: Ballantine, 2001.

Turnbull, Andrew, ed. *The Letters of F. Scott Fitzgerald.* New York: Scribners, 1963.

Turnbull, Andrew. *Scott Fitzgerald.* New York, Scribners, 1962.

West, James L. W. III. "Ginevra and Scott, Their Romance." *Princeton University Library Chronicle* 65.1 (Autumn 2003): 13–42.

ILLUSTRATION CREDITS

INDEX

JAMES L. W. WEST III is Sparks Professor of English at Pennsylvania State University. He has held fellowships from the Guggenheim Foundation, the National Humanities Center, and the National Endowment for the Humanities, and has been a Fulbright scholar to England and Belgium. He is the author of *William Styron: A Life* and is general editor of the Cambridge Edition of the Works of F. Scott Fitzgerald.

A B O U T   T H E   T Y P E

This book is set in Fournier, a typeface named for Pierre Simon Fournier, the youngest son of a French printing family. He began as an engraver of woodblocks and large capitals, then moved on to fonts of type. In 1736 he began his own foundry and made several important contributions in the field of type design; he is said to have cut 147 alphabets of his own creation. Fournier is probably best remembered as the designer of St. Augustine Ordinaire, a face that served as the model for Monotype's Fournier, which was released in 1925.